Early praise for Michelle L. Whitlock and
How I Lost My Uterus and Found My Voice

"Engaging, smart, and intimate. *How I Lost My Uterus and Found My Voice* offers a rare, personal view into a young woman's world, when her fertility and future are threatened by cancer. Michelle's story gives hope to those facing a life-threatening diagnosis while juggling a budding career, new relationships, and dreams for starting a family. You won't put it down."

—Marcia Donziger, MyLifeLine.org Cancer Foundation

"Michelle has a compelling story that will move and inspire. She shares her journey in her memoir, *How I Lost My Uterus and Found My Voice,* from stirrups to survivor with an unedited honesty and humor that will make you cringe, cry, laugh, and then jump fully into life."

—Christine Baze, executive director of the Yellow Umbrella Organization

"Michelle Whitlock has an *amazing* way of sharing her deep and personal experience to motivate, inspire, and teach others that somehow, some way, good things result from life's biggest challenges. In her memoir, *How I Lost My Uterus and Found My Voice,* she illustrates to us that this is how we all need to live: fight like hell and expect to win big!"

—Jonny Immerman, founder of Immerman Angels

"*How I Lost My Uterus and Found My Voice* is a must read for all women. Michelle has a profound way of telling her story, taking a delicate topic and infusing witty humor throughout, making it something we can all relate to! Michelle's words, wrapped in passion, will make you laugh, cry, and cheer."

—Marybeth Hammer, musician and founder of Concerts for a Cure

"*How I Lost My Uterus and Found My Voice* is an example of how the power of faith, trust, hope, and love far outweighs loss and fear. Michelle's story is about transformation and how strength is on the flip side of vulnerability. Empowering, inspiring, and filled with witty humor, this is a book you won't put down."

—Selma Schimmel, CEO and founder of Vital Options International and The Group Room® cancer talk show host

"*How I Lost My Uterus and Found My Voice* will move you to the core and help stir and awaken your inner power to fight. Michelle weaves witty humor, raw honesty, and love into her words, illustrating how a cancer survivor can get through the pain and loss of diagnosis and treatment. Michelle's authentic view on how it feels to experience cervical cancer is balanced with her positive perspective about health, love, and trust."

—Allison Hicks, Cervical Cancer Survivor, founder and executive director of The Hicks Foundation

"Michelle Whitlock takes readers through a journey of loss and love and ends up giving a blueprint on how to make a comeback. *How I Lost My Uterus and Found My Voice* will make you laugh and cry and leave you wanting more. There will be no pages left unturned in this deeply personal memoir. This book isn't just for those who have survived cancer—it's for the masses. *How I Lost My Uterus and Found My Voice* is a thrilling look at life."

—Tamika Felder, founder of Tamika & Friends, Inc.
Together Fighting Cervical Cancer

"*How I Lost My Uterus and Found My Voice*, Michelle's memoir of her journey through cervical cancer, is inspirational and educational! I was swept along with the emotion portrayed in this poignant story that every woman must read."

—Kellie Delveaux, cofounder of SAS Cervical Cancer Foundation

"*How I Lost My Uterus and Found My Voice* serves as an inspiration to the many women living with cancer. Michelle's story emphasizes the importance of continued surveillance and choosing a gynecologic oncologist if a gynecologic cancer is suspected or diagnosed."

—Karen J. Carlson, executive director of the Foundation for Women's Cancer (formerly the Gynecologic Cancer Foundation)

"Michelle is a heroine in the fight against cervical cancer. Her courage reminds me of my daughter Kristen's battle, but with a much better outcome. Her determination to live a normal life while riding the roller coaster of cancer is a wonderful encouragement to all women. Her willingness to share her story in *How I Lost My Uterus and Found My Voice* is priceless and inspirational."

—Kirk Forbes, author of *Love, Kristen*

"Michelle Whitlock writes a deeply moving, personal account of her own experience with cervical cancer. Her memoir, *How I Lost My Uterus and Found My Voice,* is brave, touching, and passionate. A highly recommended read for all women."

—Jennifer S. Smith, associate professor at the UNC Gillings School of Global Public Health and director of Cervical Cancer-Free America

"Thankfully, Michelle Whitlock found her voice and has shared it with the world. Her inspiring memoir, *How I Lost My Uterus and Found My Voice,* reads like a fast paced mystery—every unfolding detail makes you hang on to the edge of your seat! Michelle's honest account of finding courage, laughter, hope, and love where the C word once hung like a life sentence will make you *not* want to put this book down!"

—Alice Crisci, author of *Too Young for This* and founder of Fertile Action

Awards for Michelle L. Whitlock and
How I Lost My Uterus and Found My Voice

Winner: Women's Issues, *Indie Reader Discovery Award, 2013*

Winner: Women's Health, *Indie Excellence Award, 2012*

Winner, Gold Medal: Non-Fiction Memoir, *Reader's Favorite, 2012*

Finalist: Health--Women's Health, *The 2012 USA Best Book Awards, 2012*

Finalist: Autobiography, *Next Generation Indie Book Awards, 2012*

Finalist: Memoir (Overcoming Adversity/Tragedy/Challenge), *Next Generation Indie Book Awards, 2012*

Finalist: Women's Issues, *Next Generation Indie Book Awards, 2012*

Honorable Mention: Autobiography/Biograpghy, *Los Angeles Book Festival, 2012*

Editor's Choice Award: *iUniverse, 2011*

Rising Star Award: *iUniverse, 2011*

How I Lost My Uterus and Found My Voice

A Memoir of Love, Hope, and Empowerment

Michelle L. Whitlock

Edited by Erin Essenmacher
Cover Photo by Tracy Friend

iUniverse

How I Lost My Uterus and Found My Voice
A Memoir of Love, Hope, and Empowerment

The information, ideas, and suggestions in this book are not intended as a substitute for professional medical advice. Before following any suggestions contained in this book, you should consult your personal physician. Neither the author nor the publisher shall be liable or responsible for any loss or damage allegedly arising as a consequence of your use or application of any information or suggestions in this book.

iUniverse Star
an iUniverse LLC imprint

iUniverse books may be ordered through booksellers or by contacting:

iUniverse
1663 Liberty Drive
Bloomington, IN 47403
www.iuniverse.com
1-800-Authors (1-800-288-4677)

Because of the dynamic nature of the Internet, any Web addresses or links contained in this book may have changed since publication and may no longer be valid. The views expressed in this work are solely those of the author and do not necessarily reflect the views of the publisher, and the publisher hereby disclaims any responsibility for them.

Any people depicted in stock imagery provided by Thinkstock are models, and such images are being used for illustrative purposes only. Certain stock imagery © Thinkstock.

ISBN: 978-1-4917-7145-7 (sc)
ISBN: 978-1-4917-7146-4 (e)

Library of Congress Control Number: 2015911080

Print information available on the last page.

iUniverse rev. date: 8/28/2015

For my girls:
Riley Grier
Savvy Rose
Shelby-Kay
Cassidy Sommerlyn
Anna Grace
Emalee Michelle
Amy Jo
Adelyn Grace

There's a long, long trail a-winding
Into the land of my dreams
Where the nightingales are singing
And a white moon beams:
There's a long, long night of waiting
Until my dreams all come true;
Till the day when I'll be going down
That long, long trail with you.

—Stoddard King
(Sung as a lullaby to me by my grandma)

Contents

Introduction   xvii

Part 1. The Pivotal Week   1

Turning Point   2
April 2004

Part 2. Everything Before   11

Initiation   12
Fall 1992

Chance Encounter   19
June 2001

Fireworks   30
July 2001

Feminine Itch   34
July 2001

Magic Words   37
August 2001

Trouble on the Horizon   41
October to November 2001

The Breakup   47
December 2001

Results   50
December 2001

The Getaway   56
    December 2001

Reality   60
    December 2001 to January 2002

Research   65
    January 2002

Options   71
    January 2002

Surgery   76
    February 2002

Healing   80
    March 2002 to May 2003

Part 3. Everything After   85

The Morning After   86
    April 2004

Coping   90
    May 2004

Maybe Babies   95
    May to June 2004

Jamaican Wedding   104
    June 2004

Dreaded Surgery   114
    June 2004

Another Crack 121
July 2004

Decisions 124
July 2004

(Another) Health Insurance Nightmare 126
July 2004

Heavy Artillery 128
August to September 2004

Aftermath 141
September to December 2004

New Beginnings 148
Winter to summer 2005

Reclaiming My Sexuality 154
Fall 2005 to spring 2006

Two-Year Checkup, Round Two 156
August 2006

Finding My Voice 160
Late 2006 to early 2007

Prayers 163
Spring 2007

Epilogue 165

HPV and Cervical Cancer Facts 169

Tips to My Girlfriends 173

Resource Directory 177

Acknowledgements

As this is a work of non-fiction, I have recreated the conversations to the best of my ability, using my memory, personal notes, journals, medical charts, and interviews with loved ones. With their permissions, I have chosen not to change most of the people's names, due to the deep and personal relationships I have with them. One exception is medical personnel, whom I shall refer to with only a single letter out of respect for their privacy and practices.

To Mark: my husband, best friend, lover, and angel. Thank you for sharing this life with me daily. Your love is the best medicine around.

I began writing as part of my healing process and had no intention of ever sharing it publicly. However, each time I talked about it with my husband, he encouraged me to keep writing and—as a proud husband does—he boasted about my writing to friends, family members, and colleagues. His sharing sparked curiosity in other women. I found myself overwhelmed by their interest, questions, and willingness to discuss their own experiences. Often, hearing my story gave these women the encouragement needed to share their stories for the first time.

The more women I talked to, the more I realized that each of us has had a unique experience—from the uncomfortable gyn visit to the abnormal Pap test to the "I didn't know" lesson—but not all of us were talking about them. In fact, as evolved as I thought we women were, many of us were still very hush-hush about feminine issues and concerns. That subject was still taboo in many circles. Since having sex, going to the gynecologist, and dealing with feminine issues are all a natural part of womanhood, I decided it was time to speak out. There was no need to whisper about these subjects or talk only behind closed doors. I felt inspired to write more, and I published a few articles at the suggestion of one of my husband's clients.

I'd like to thank my family—those I'm tied to through biology and those who I've chosen as my family—for your love, support, and encouragement. I have been blessed with the best girlfriends a girl could ever ask for: I love you, Andi, Brooke, Caryn, Cathy, Halle, Janis, Janelle, Kristen, Kristi, Laura,

Tracy, and Trista. Alex, you are the best; thank you for being here. A special thanks to Caryn for proofing my earliest drafts and providing me with true, honest feedback, and to Alex, Brooke, Heather, and Halle. I couldn't have finished this project without you.

To my writer friends Cindy, Jacqueline, and Wendy: I am so appreciative of the advice and guidance you offered so freely, even when I didn't agree.

Helaine and Tracy: I can't express how much I have learned and grown while working with you. Thank you for the opportunities and friendship. I am a better advocate today because of the experience I have had with you.

Erin, my editor and friend—isn't life funny? When I started this book, I had no idea it would somehow lead me back to you. I believe people are brought into our path for a reason, and so it is fitting that you, my best childhood friend, would reappear after nearly twelve years, just in time to help me shape the flow of my memoir. When we started collaborating on this project, I thought it was done. Boy, was I wrong. Thank you for challenging me and for asking the probing questions that helped to fill in the gaps and polish my story. At times in my life, you knew me better than anyone, yet our distance over the last decade has given you the objectivity that I needed to complete this project. Your unique and creative perspective made all the difference. Thank you for helping make this dream a reality.

Kacey, your integrity and work ethic stretch above and beyond. You are a master at the English language—my own personal Jedi! It was such a pleasure working with you and learning from you. Although we have never set eyes on each other, I feel like we have been friends for a lifetime.

Kristi and Evelyn, my first survivor sisters: thank you for opening up and allowing me to feel understood. You gave me hope in my darkest hours and you showed me the power in sharing and connecting with others.

Allison, Christine, and Tamika: each of you took an enormous tragedy in your life and transformed it into a beacon of light for other women. My survivor sisters are a daily inspiration to me, and I thank you for the work you do every day to educate other women. I am grateful for all the women who fought the battle against cervical cancer and won. I honor those who lost the fight, and I express my gratitude to the men who loved these ladies before, during, and after their journey.

And finally, in memory of my grandmother, Dr. Mary Lou Sweet Anderson, who taught me to stand strong and persevere. I love you more than words can ever say. Thank you for choosing to be my mother.

Life is a series of choices. For better or worse, they are ours to make and they give shape to our existence. Thank you all for choosing to be a part of my life and journey.

Introduction

Where does a story begin? Where does it end? As I sat to write about my journey and how it changed the course of my life, I struggled with these questions. Again and again, I found my mind drifting back to a college English assignment in which the professor asked me to write about the ten most influential or defining moments that shaped my life. Of course, I wrote that paper long before the majority of these events took place. But that exercise helped set the stage for the beginning of this book. In my long journey through the hell of HPV and cervical cancer, one particular week stood out above all others. I decided to start my story during that week and called it Part I. Those emotionally charged seven days seemed to divide my entire cancer experience into two parts: everything that came before (which I've included in Part II of this book) and everything that came after (which I've written about in Part III). I know it may seem unconventional to start in the middle of my story chronologically, and then to skip back in time in Part II and forward in time for Part III; but narratively, it felt right to launch from the point that shaped the course of my life. It perfectly encapsulated all that had happened and all that was about to unfold.

Looking back on that pivotal week, I also realized *why* I wanted to tell this story. We all go through those awkward teen years, when we are still adolescents but experiencing adult feelings. All those raging hormones catapult us into a new realm of sexuality, in which we try to figure out what feels right and how and when to express it. Most of us lack the foresight to see how our early sexual decisions—and every one that follows—can affect the rest of our lives. The fact that few adults seem to be willing to acknowledge that teens are having sex only deepens the confusion. The reluctance to talk about sex and sexual health doesn't go away as we get older. Now that I know firsthand the consequences of not talking about it, I think something needs to change.

The American Cancer Society reports that about 500,000 women worldwide are diagnosed with cervical cancer annually. More than 250,000 of them die from the disease. Even in a developed country like the United States, approximately 12,000 women are diagnosed with this preventable disease every year, and one third of them die. We now know cervical cancer is caused by certain strains of the sexually transmitted human papillomavirus, commonly called HPV.

Consider this: according to the Centers for Disease Control and Prevention, approximately seventy-nine million Americans are currently infected with HPV. Another fourteen million people become newly infected each year. HPV is so common that *almost all* sexually active men and women get it at some point in their lives. And while not everyone who has sex or contracts HPV will get cancer, millions of American women do have abnormal Pap tests annually. The treatment for abnormal Pap tests and cervical cancer can affect a woman's ability to bear children.

Just hearing the words "abnormal" and "Pap" in the same sentence can feel scary and isolating to a woman, but it can become downright paralyzing when she then considers whether or not to tell a parent, a friend, a friend-with-benefits, a boyfriend, a spouse—or anyone else, for that matter. An HPV diagnosis can make dating overwhelming and confusing: Do I have to tell a partner I have or had HPV? When do I tell? Can I still be intimate and engage in sexual activity? For those already in a relationship, additional concerns arise. Some are left to wonder if they contracted HPV from their partner, while others worry that if their beloved finds out about the diagnosis, he/she might leave. Any couple confronted with an illness inevitably faces the age-old concern: Can love truly survive both in sickness and in health? While I don't have all the answers to these questions, I do have my own experience to share as a guide.

I want everyone who reads this book to know two things: you are not alone, and we absolutely must start talking about sex and sexual health. Parents, think back, did you phone home for permission to experiment with sex? I know, I didn't and while I hope your children will, the reality is most teens and young adults will not ask for permission before engaging in sexual activity. It takes only one sexual encounter, with or without a condom to get a STD that could affect the rest of your life. No matter what your age, if you are having sex or sexual contact—and let's face it, most of us are—you are at risk for coming into contact with HPV. I want women everywhere to be empowered, to open up and talk freely and fearlessly about their bodies, sexual experiences, and sexual health. Your life and reproductive future, or the life and reproductive future of someone close to you, just might depend on it. And yes, it is possible to still have a fulfilling, romantic relationship after a diagnosis of HPV and/or cancer. *So if you have a vagina or love someone with a vagina, this book is for you.*

PART I
The Pivotal Week

April 2004

Turning Point ————————————————————

April 2004

This can't be happening. Not again. Not now.

I sat straight up, sweat dripping from my forehead, startled by what had become a recurring nightmare. I wiped the sleep from my eyes. *It's just a dream*, I realized as I got out of bed, trying to shake the fear.

It was Friday, April 16, 2004, and that time again. It happened every three months like clockwork, despite my best efforts to ignore it. Most women only make an annual trip to the gynecologist, but not me. As a twenty-nine-year-old cervical cancer survivor, I visited my gynecological oncologist at the change of every season. I hated these appointments—the poking, the prodding. No matter how many times I went, it never got easier. This day marked two years since I had been declared cancer free. I should have been celebrating, but I was actually dreading this appointment even more than usual. My annual exams, like the one today, were more extensive than the quarterly checkups. Plus, my doctor took extra precautions, given my cancer history. To treat my cancer, I had opted for a controversial procedure she wouldn't ever have recommended, but now the burden was on her to ensure that my cancer didn't return.

I tried to take my mind off the appointment by focusing on work. I was an assistant district manager for a national shoe retail chain, which is just a polite way of saying district manager-in-training, or as my boss said, "Ain't a district manager yet." I was reading yet another e-mail when I heard the humming of the garage door opening. Mark, my boyfriend of three years, walked in and called up to me, "Honey, I'm home. Are you ready to go?"

"Be right there," I yelled.

"Hurry. We're going to be late!"

I jumped up and raced down the stairs to meet him. "Let me just grab the medicine she prescribed. I'll meet you at the car."

I grabbed the pills and a coke—my one vice in this world—before I headed for the car. As I settled into the passenger seat, Mark asked, "What are those and why are you taking them?"

"One is Lortab for pain, and the other is Valium to help me relax so the procedure will go more smoothly." I added playfully, "That's why you need to drive, mister."

The medicine kicked in about twenty minutes later, as we arrived at the clinic. I reached for Mark's arm and held on as we passed through the doorway. We signed in, sat down, and waited for my name to be called.

Finally, I heard the nurse say, "Michelle Coots?"

Only professional people called me Michelle. My friends and family knew me as Michi, pronounced Mickey, like the mouse.

The nurse directed me to the scale for the usual height and weight measurements. I kicked off my heels and stood against the wall. As usual I measured five feet, seven and a half inches. I always wished I were an inch or two taller, which is why I have to include the half. It's also why I almost always wear heels. I stepped onto the scale: 130 pounds.

The nurse escorted Mark and me into the examination room and continued to take the usual vital statistics. "Dr. C. will be in shortly," she said as she walked out.

I didn't need any instructions; I was a pro and knew the drill. I undressed from the waist down and positioned myself on the examination table with the always flattering white sheet draped over my lower half. The next few minutes seemed like an eternity as I sat half-naked, freezing my buns off, waiting for the doctor. I was beginning to feel like I had downed a bottle of wine. *Oh, yeah, the medicine is definitely kicking in now!*

When Dr. C. entered the room, she began with the usual battery of questions. "How are you feeling? Has anything changed?" Blah, blah, blah. Then she made her normal plea: "You make me so nervous. I wish you would just get pregnant and let me remove your uterus so we can be sure you're in the clear."

Dr. C. was the third in a string of oncologists that had been in charge of my follow-up care since the dreaded diagnosis two and a half years ago. Each doctor had recommended a hysterectomy, and every time, I had refused. I didn't know if I wanted children, but I knew I was not ready to give up my ability to make that choice. Instead, I had chosen a nontraditional procedure—a radical trachelectomy—to treat the cervical cancer. The doctors had removed a large portion of my cervix, but had left my uterus intact. Dr. C. was not a fan of my chosen course of treatment. She felt the radical trachelectomy was too new, that the overall long-term success rate was too uncertain. This was also the reason my annual checkups involved more than the traditional Pap test. She wanted to track my recovery closely because she was skeptical that my cancer was really gone for good.

"Okay, are you ready, Michelle?"

"Ready as I am going to be," I said, reaching for Mark's hand.

"Slide down a little farther," she instructed, as she made a tent with the white sheet over my knees. Even though I had done this a thousand times, those words always made my stomach queasy. I couldn't think of a more vulnerable or awkward situation than lying with my bare butt exposed to the world, having a near stranger poking around inside my most private and personal spot. Reluctantly, I slid down until I felt the end of the table. *I hate this position!*

"Okay, this is going to be a little cold and you're going to feel me insert the speculum. Now I am going to open it up. How are you doing?"

"Fine." *But not really.*

"Okay, I need to numb the area with local anesthetic. Take a deep breath and hold it in. You are going to feel the prick of the needle and a little burning sensation."

As the needle penetrated the base of my uterus, where my cervix used to be, I felt the instant burn of the medicine. I had taken the Lortab, but the pain came anyway. My body tightened, and I clenched Mark's hand as I gasped for another breath.

"Are you still with me?" Dr. C. asked.

"Yeah," I mumbled.

"Remember, deep, slow breaths."

I didn't respond. I was too busy focusing on my breathing so I wouldn't knock her over and flee the room.

"Okay," she said, "two more quick sticks. Now we'll wait a few minutes and give the anesthetic time to take effect."

My head felt fuzzy and my eyes were heavy. Those few minutes felt like hours. Finally Dr. C. checked to ensure that the area inside me was numb. Once she was confident that it was, she proceeded with a wet Pap.

"I want to take an extra step today," she said when she was done with the Pap. "It's called an endocervical curettage, or ECC, and it will help ensure that there's no new cancer present."

She talked me through the procedure as she went, explaining that she was making a small incision at the base of the uterus. Next, she inserted a spoon-shaped tool into the incision. She scraped around the interior walls where the uterus and the upper end of the vaginal canal had been sewn together after my last surgery. I breathed in and gnashed my teeth in a feeble attempt to counter the extreme discomfort. A few blessed moments later, she finished and instructed me to get dressed.

"The results should take about two weeks," she said. "Assuming everything is okay, I shouldn't need to see you for another four months."

An extra month of freedom! I was elated with this news.

Mark helped me to the car. Between the medicine and the stomach cramps from the procedure, I was ready to get the hell out of there and home to my bed. I knew Mark had made dinner plans, but they would have to wait until the drugs wore off. Once we got home, I fell asleep quickly and snoozed for several hours.

I awoke still a little foggy from the medicine. "Hello, sleepyhead," Mark teased as I struggled to adjust my eyes to the bright overhead light. "Ready for our big night out?"

"Can't I have just a few more minutes?" I pleaded.

"Not a chance, baby. I've been planning this all week! Get those pretty baby blues open and your feet on the ground. I'll start your shower."

He turned on the water in the bathroom. Starting my shower was part of our usual morning drill. I hated leaving the comfort of my warm, snuggly sheets and being smacked in the face with the cool air from the air conditioner. A hot shower was one of the tricks Mark had learned to get my ass out of bed. I climbed in and let the water cascade over me. As I stood there with my eyes closed, I sighed as the tension of the day washed down the drain with the water.

Mark's voice snapped me out of my reverie. "Hurry up! Our reservation is at eight. We need to leave in thirty minutes, hot lips. Chop, chop!"

I got out of the shower and sat down on the vanity stool in front of the mirror. Growing up in a dysfunctional family, I had learned to cultivate a tough exterior, to guard my vulnerabilities. In some ways, my makeup was like my armor. It was my way of choosing which version of me the world would see. With each stroke of the brush, I covered my visible imperfections, the ones that might leave me exposed, might make me seem less in the eyes of another. But it was more than that. I had grown up with a single dad who raised me the best way he knew how. However, let's just say that he wasn't into lipstick and eye shadow, so I missed out on a lot of the feminine rituals most girls shared with their mothers. Even now, thirty-odd years later, the girly stuff—picking out clothes and applying makeup—felt like such a treat that I liked to take my time with it.

After applying the requisite color to my cheeks and the perfect shade of mauve to make my blue eyes "pop," I quickly used the blow-dryer on my shoulder-length red hair. I had always had a thing for loud, attention-grabbing red hair, so I went and got some. I slipped into my favorite jeans, a low-cut cotton shirt, and three-inch wedge heels. I took one final look in the mirror just as Mark poked his head in the door.

"Any day now!" he said, grinning.

I grabbed my bag and off we went.

Thirty minutes later we arrived at our favorite restaurant, ready to chow down on some the best Thai food Memphis had to offer. The hostess recognized us immediately and greeted us with a hug. Since the restaurant was packed, she asked us to wait at the bar.

Mark and I perched on stools and ordered two glasses of pinot grigio. As we enjoyed our wine, I found myself lost in thought, staring at the mirror hanging over the bar. The visit to the doctor weighed heavily on my mind. I tried each day to live my life in the present and to forget that I had even had cancer, but the appointment that day had brought all the memories rushing back. I couldn't help but wonder what my future held. *What will I look like as an old woman? Will I even get to be an old woman?*

I turned to Mark and asked, "What do you think I will look like in fifty years?"

He chuckled, but then he got a serious look on his face. He told me how much he loved me and loved our life together. He said he didn't think he could love me any more than he loved me at that moment, whether we were married or not. I wasn't sure what he was saying, but something told me it wasn't good. Mark had broken up with me once before, at a time when I was sure things were going great between us. *Oh, no. Not again. Is he trying to tell me that he loves me but never wants to get married? Or is this another attempt to break it off by letting me down easy?* My heart began to beat faster, and I felt like a brick had dropped into the pit of my stomach. As I sat in silence, avoiding looking at him, I felt my eyes grow heavy with the weight of oncoming tears.

Of course Mark noticed the change in my expression and instantly asked what was wrong.

"Nothing, I'm fine," I said, which really meant that everything was wrong and, no, I wouldn't talk about it.

Mark tried to get me to open up. "Baby, please talk to me."

I resisted. I just didn't want to get into it. I stared at the ceiling, an old trick I used to fight back tears. Finally, I broke. "If you didn't want to marry me, you could have told me months ago. You let me think our relationship was leading to something more." Mark tried to interrupt, but I cut him off and continued. "I was fine before, thinking we would never get married, but then lately you started talking about marriage and got my hopes up. Hell, Mark, you even took me to the bookstore to look at wedding vows." By now the tears, mixed with black mascara, flowed down my cheeks.

"No, baby," Mark said, "you have it all wrong. Will you marry me?"

I felt my face heat with an angry flush. "No. Don't patronize me by asking me now."

Mark slid his stool back from the bar. "I am really serious. Will you marry me? I was trying to ask you all along. I brought you here to propose!"

He went down on his knee and asked a third time. "Will you marry me?

"Mark, stand up and stop this! People are looking at us!"

He stood and placed his hand in his pocket. "What do I have to do, pull out a ring?"

I looked down at his hand, which held a sparkling round diamond set in a beautiful gold band. I was speechless.

It finally dawned on me that he wasn't kidding. "Yes, of course," I shouted as I threw my arms around him.

The sound of wild applause filled the restaurant just as the hostess came over to seat us. Over a dinner of green curry and rice, we laughed and joked about the catastrophe that Mark's proposal had almost become. I had truly thought he was telling me that he never wanted to marry me.

That night as we drove home, I pulled out my cell phone and called everyone I could think of to share our news. I couldn't believe we were actually getting married!

The next morning, Saturday, as I began to talk about wedding plans, Mark set a few ground rules. He wanted a barefoot beach wedding and our own vows. He rejected traditional vows in favor of something more personal: a passage from the book *Conversations with God* by Neale Donald Walsch. My only stipulation was the date: June 18, the anniversary of the night we met. It just so happened that we already had a beach getaway planned for that date. Every June for the past three years, we had taken a trip to celebrate our anniversary. This year, we had plans to vacation in Negril, Jamaica. The aptly named Couple's Resort had come highly recommended by a colleague and close friend of mine. When we had made the reservation several months earlier, I had had no idea we'd be getting married, but now it seemed like a no-brainer. Our beach vacation would be the perfect time and place to make it all official.

Once we agreed on Jamaica, we jumped out of bed and ran upstairs to the computer. Mark typed "Couples Resort Jamaica" into the browser line, and within a few minutes we had all the answers we needed to arrange our wedding. We sent an e-mail to the resort's wedding coordinator, reserving our date and requesting the last ceremony of the day. (The sun setting over the ocean would make the perfect backdrop.) The rest of that day and most of the next was consumed with wedding talk, and before we knew it, it was time to get back to our busy work schedules.

The start of the week was a total blur. I was covering for the district manager who was out of town, which meant double the workload. I didn't even know where Monday and Tuesday went. Wednesday, however, was a long day—eleven hours to be exact—but I didn't mind because I was still on cloud nine. In fact, I was so wrapped up in engagement bliss, I had completely forgotten about my visit to the doctor the week before.

I pulled into the driveway a little before nine Wednesday night and noticed that Mark was not home yet. As usual, when I opened the door, our dogs George and Charlee came running, wagging their tails and covering me in wet kisses.

As I kicked off my shoes, I noticed the answering machine light blinking red. I didn't check the message immediately. Instead, I began my evening ritual of running a hot bath in our large Jacuzzi-style tub. I undressed, dropped my clothes on the floor, and turned on the water.

While I waited for the tub to fill, I called our voice mail. I assumed the message was from a telemarketer. Anyone who knew us, knew Mark and I didn't answer the house phone and seldom checked the messages. If our friends wanted to reach us, they called our cell phones. I dialed in and heard the robotic greeter say, "You have one new message." I pressed the button and heard a familiar voice. "Michelle, this is Dr. C. Please give me a call back at the office as soon as you get this message."

My mouth dropped open as the phone slipped from my hand and crashed to the floor. I stood there frozen, unable to compose myself. The message was short, but it spoke volumes. Instinctively, I reached down and picked up the phone. I don't remember dialing, but before I knew it I could hear Mark's voice on the other end of the line.

"Michi? Michi? Hello? What's going on?"

With my voice trembling, I simply said, "I have cancer—again."

"What? What are you talking about? That's crazy!"

"Dr. C. called and left a message on the machine today."

"Well, what did she say?"

"Nothing. Just to give her a call at the office."

"That's it, that's all? Okay, so she wants you to call. That doesn't mean anything. Why are you so freaked out? I'm sure it's nothing. We'll call her first thing tomorrow."

"No! You don't understand. If everything was fine her nurse, Robin, would have called with the results, or they would have sent me a postcard saying, 'Everything is okay. See you in four months.'"

"Maybe Robin was busy and Dr. C. decided to make the call herself. Don't you think you're jumping to conclusions?"

"No. Dr. C. would only make the call if something was wrong. I am telling you, I have cancer again!"

"Michi, calm down. I am going to be home in about ten minutes. Why don't you get into your tub and try to chill out for a minute? I will see you as fast as I can get back to the house."

I slid into the hot water and rested my head against the back of the tub, shell-shocked. It probably took Mark thirty minutes to get home, but it felt like hours. He immediately joined me in the bathroom, sitting Indian-style on the floor. We replayed the same conversation several times, before I finally told him I wanted to be alone for a while. I knew Mark was just being logical, but I had been around this block before and deep in my gut I just knew.

No, no, no, this can't be happening! Not now. He finally proposed. I am making wedding plans. It's my turn for the fairy tale, for the happily ever after. This just can't be. I cannot have cancer again … especially not now.

I closed my eyes and recalled the journey we had already taken, from the day we met to this moment.

PART II
Everything Before

Fall 1992 to May 2003

Initiation

Fall 1992

So many times when you hear stories about women who get cervical cancer, inevitably it comes out that they missed a Pap test or hadn't had one in years. That was never the case with me. I've always been good about getting my annual gynecological exam. Even when I was diagnosed with cancer, my Pap was completely normal. In fact, my only abnormal Pap test happened back in 1992, when I was seventeen.

It was my second annual exam, and to say that I didn't much care for the procedure would be an understatement. It felt weird to lie on the table, naked from the waist down, totally exposed with my feet in those funny stirrups.

The nurse called me a few days later with the results. I heard "abnormal" and didn't understand anything else she told me. I began to cry hysterically. I thought she was telling me that I had cancer and was going to die. I hung up the phone and ran to my father, still sobbing. He was clueless, too, but he wanted to comfort me, so he pretended he understood exactly what I was talking about.

My dad, Jim, raised my two sisters and me with the help of his mother after my mom left us to head out on the road as a truck driver. I was three years old when she left, and for years after that, we only saw our mother on the rare occasions when a load brought her through town. My dad did his best to make up for her absence, such as learning to braid my waist-length hair. But there are some things for which a girl needs a mother, and despite his best efforts, I was starting to have life experiences that my dad couldn't relate to. This was one of them.

I went in the week after the abnormal Pap to see Dr. T. She tried to explain the meaning of the test to me. "No, you don't have cancer! The abnormal result means you have low-grade dysplasia."

L to R; Lori, Me, Shawna and Mom in her tractor trailer

L to R; Me, Daddy and Lori

I nodded as if I knew what that was, but I didn't. I later learned that it meant some of the cells on my cervix had changed. They weren't cancerous, but they weren't normal either, and they needed to be removed. It was a common diagnosis requiring a simple treatment, but to me it felt like the end of the world. She gave me a pamphlet on abnormal Pap tests to read and set up an appointment. She mentioned that possible causes included having sex at an early age and having the human papillomavirus (HPV). I didn't know what HPV was and I didn't ask any questions about it either. *She's the expert, after all,* I told myself, *and she only mentioned possible causes. It doesn't mean I have a disease.*

In her office a few days later, Dr. T. performed the procedure. My dad offered to accompany me, but he was the last person I wanted there. Instead I chose the girl who had been my best friend since the seventh grade. Erin knew all my secrets; she wasn't going to judge me. Plus she had a uterus and a vagina, so I figured she could relate. She followed me back to see Dr. T. and promised to hold my hand the entire time. As we entered the room, the first thing I saw was a complex, scary looking blue medical chair fitted with metal stirrups. *What in the world is that?* I was sure I was about to find out, and that's what worried me.

Reluctantly, I followed the nurse's orders and undressed from the waist down, and then sat in the menacing blue chair and positioned my feet in the stirrups. When the doctor was ready, the chair began to recline backward. Once I was almost flat on my back, the seat dropped out, exposing my butt to both the doctor and the frigid room.

She inserted a speculum, opening the vaginal canal. She then applied liquid nitrogen to my cervix in order to freeze and destroy the abnormal cells. "You'll feel some pressure and cramping," she said. "Take deep breaths."

Pressure? It felt more like someone had punched me in the crotch.

The whole process lasted only a few minutes, but it felt like an eternity. "No sex!" Dr. T. ordered as I left the office. I nodded numbly. Sex was pretty much the last thing on my mind. My stomach cramped, and I could feel a nasty discharge filling my panties.

It would continue that way for the next few weeks. *The joys of being a woman,* I thought. I was only seventeen, and in a lot of ways I still felt like a kid, but here I was having a very adult experience without my mom to guide me.

My boyfriend at the time was also seventeen and even more clueless than I was. I didn't fully understand what was happening to me, so I didn't even bother trying to explain it to him. I avoided being alone with him during the few weeks I was healing. I didn't want to talk about what had happened at the doctor's or feel pressured to have sex.

Erin and me in a photo booth being silly

When I learned to ride a bike as a small child, I fell a time or two and scraped my knees. Those tumbles scared me initially, but I always got back on the bike. Eventually, I figured it out, and the fear of falling was replaced by the sweet sensation of freedom.

As a teenager, my hormones ran wild. Sexual temptation seemed to lurk around every corner, beckoning me. My initial experiences with boys reminded me of learning to ride a bike, and this experience with my abnormal Pap test was like that first fall. It totally freaked me out, but the fear was short-lived. As the physical pain and unpleasant side effects diminished, so did the memory of the ordeal and the fear associated with it. Within no time I started seeing my boyfriend again, exploring his body, learning mine, and generally giving in to those raging hormonal impulses.

Dr. T., on the other hand, had not forgotten. The abnormal cells triggered enough concern that she set me up for a repeat Pap test every four months for the next year. Luckily, they were all normal, which meant I could go back to a regular schedule of having just one Pap test a year. I was elated with the news and all too happy to put the entire experience behind me, but one lesson did hit home: I never missed an annual Pap test after that.

I was able to hold onto that blissful ignorance for the next seven years, until early 2000, right around the time I turned twenty-five. That was when I learned about HPV and its potentially destructive effects. It all started out innocently enough. I went to Dr. T. complaining of mild external itching down south. The area was red from my incessant scratching, but otherwise it looked normal. I didn't have any weird smell or discharge, so I was sure it wasn't an STD.

It took three separate visits before Dr. T. discovered the cause of my discomfort. The first two times she examined me, she couldn't find anything abnormal. She gave me a hydrocortisone cream to help with the itching and sent me home. The third time many weeks later, she decided to swab my vulva and perform a small biopsy.

A few days later I was told that as with those worrisome cervical cells seven years earlier, these cells had come back abnormal.

How could that be? I wondered. *And what exactly does "abnormal" mean?*

The clinical term was VIN II and III—more dysplasia, but this time she said the cells were pre-cancerous. Dr. T. explained that the changes were most likely due to the HPV virus. All I knew about HPV was that it had something to do with genital warts.

What I didn't realize then was that one didn't need to be promiscuous to get HPV. A single sexual encounter was all it took. Still, hearing those words made me feel dirty.

"I don't have warts!" I shouted defensively.

"I know, honey," she said. "I don't think you understand."

She explained that HPV was the most common sexually transmitted virus, and while it could cause vaginal warts in some cases, there were over one hundred strains. Each strain caused different symptoms, and each person was affected differently. Most women never even knew they had HPV. Their immune systems fought the virus, and it cleared up on its own. In other cases, cells of the vulva or cervix changed and became abnormal. Left untreated, those abnormal cells could become cancerous. I didn't know exactly what she was telling me, but I knew it was somehow connected to cancer, and that unnerved me.

"Most women experience some cell change. It's really very normal," Dr. T. said. However, even knowing that whatever was happening to me might be "normal," I felt confused and embarrassed. Let's just say I wasn't about to run out and tell my friends.

Dr. T. explained that I needed to have surgery to remove the abnormal cells, an outpatient procedure done under general anesthesia. While I was unconscious, she removed the surface layer of skin off my vagina with a laser. This surgery was much more painful and felt more invasive than the one I had undergone at seventeen. And the pain lingered. I rotated between the couch, the tub, and my bed for the next week. Dr. T. prescribed silver nitrate burn cream to rub "down south" on the surgical site.

I used my recovery time to conduct more research and read everything I could on HPV. When I saw the doctor next, I questioned her about the possible link between the changes in my vulva and cervical cancer. Dr. T. explained that since HPV strains varied, different strains could affect different areas. Some caused changes of the cervix while others seemed to affect the vaginal canal or vulva. She said that this incident was probably not related to my previous experience. Just to be sure, she sent me to a gynecological oncologist, a cancer specialist focused on female reproductive organs. She was able to get me an appointment with Dr. A. for the following week.

I sat in Dr. A.'s waiting room for more than an hour. *Why* are *doctors always late? Is it a job requirement or something?* Eventually, the nurse called me back and led me to a room where I could wait some more. The room contained the same dreaded medical chair Dr. T. had in her office. I undressed and waited in the blue chair, covered in the usual paper sheet.

I can't believe I'm back here, stuck in this awful, butt-exposing contraption.

Finally, Dr. A. entered and quickly got down to the business at hand, reviewing my chart and asking me a few questions. He was an awkward little man with shifty eyes, much older than I, and unattractive. I felt uncomfortable talking about my sex life with this guy, especially while I was half naked.

"Are you married? Are you in a monogamous relationship? How many sexual partners have you had? Any pain with intercourse?"

The questions came at me rapid fire, each one more embarrassing than the last.

He told me more about the HPV virus. "Anyone who's been sexually intimate since the sexual revolution has come into contact with HPV, whether they know it or not. In fact, HPV is the most common STD."

So do I actually have it, and if everyone's got it, what's the big deal? I thought those questions but didn't dare ask.

Dr. A. explained that he wanted to perform a colposcopy to closely examine my vagina, inside and out. That did *not* sound fun. Sensing my hesitation, he tried to make it as easy as possible by telling me step by step exactly what he was doing. First he applied a vinegar-type solution to the cervix and the vulva. Then he inspected the area using a special tool called a colposcope, which magnified things.

"This solution will turn white on any place with possible cell changes and help identify potential problems," he explained. "If I see anything suspicious, I'll biopsy the spot."

Time stood still while I lay there with my legs spread, allowing this stranger to poke around my vagina. At this point, I had undergone more than a few Pap tests, but no matter how many times I had been through this, it never got any easier. He attempted to carry on a casual conversation with me like my hairdresser does. But I wasn't naked at the hairdresser's! I just wanted to get this over with already. I focused on taking deep breaths for the rest of the exam.

"Everything looks good," he said once he finished. "I see no reason to perform any biopsies today. Just continue following up with Dr. T. annually."

I was so relieved to be done, I threw on my pants the second he left the room and made a beeline for the door. I was more than ready to get the hell out of there and put the experience behind me. I guessed this meant I was cured. If the doctors weren't worried, why should I be?

Once again, within a few months the entire ordeal was a distant memory. I was ready to get back to my life. Besides, some of my girlfriends had had abnormal Pap tests, and they were all fine. I tried not to worry as I went to the doctor's as scheduled and had my Pap test. No doctor ever confirmed I definitely had HPV.

Chance Encounter

June 2001

I grew up in suburban Maryland, just outside of Washington, D.C. My dad was disabled and not really able to work, so we never had much money. From the time I was little, I was always the "good" daughter. As the middle child with a mostly absent mother, I quickly learned the art of pleasing the adults around me as way of controlling chaos. I played the peacemaker in my family, and was the only one of my sisters and me to do well in school.

I got my first job at a shoe store when I was seventeen. I spent my days in class and my evenings and weekends working. After graduation, many of my friends started college. I kept working. My job made me feel responsible and important. I bought a car and I was even able to help my dad with his bills. At twenty I met a nice guy and got married—one more thing off the checklist of what I was "supposed" to do. Then my dad died unexpectedly, and two years later my marriage fell apart. All of a sudden the people I had been trying to please most—my father and husband—were no longer there. I threw myself into my work full force, but I started to question how I was living my life, why, and for whom.

Around the same time, I met Janis, a friend of my younger sister. Janis was home for the holidays but lived in South Beach, Miami. We hit it off immediately, sharing stories and becoming fast friends. She gave me her number and an open invitation to visit her in paradise. Within a few months I was on a plane to Miami and almost immediately fell in love with the place.

In South Beach I was able to break out of the straitjacket of responsibility I had created for myself. There were no expectations to live up to and no other people to please. I loved the feeling of absolute freedom and I wanted more.

I had a job in retail management, and for the next two and a half years I took every opportunity I could to escape the hustle and bustle of work. I visited Janis at least every other month, sometimes more often, for four-day weekends. Janis lived completely in the moment, with a carefree abandon. Her attitude was contagious. Those trips to Miami were important to me because they represented not only a break from my work life, but also a break

19

from my reality and a chance to reinvent myself. The type-A personality that everyone knew back home transformed into a carefree, adventurous, fly-by-the-seat-of-my-pants chick as soon as my feet touched the ground at the Miami International Airport. I nicknamed this new part of myself Miami Michi because it was such a departure from my personality back in Maryland. I stayed up all night, ate in the best restaurants, and hit all the hot clubs. I felt alive in a way that I never had before.

I could only keep up the jet-setting lifestyle for so long. As much as I loved to explore this other side of my personality, the travel, the late nights, and the lack of sleep started to take a toll. When I returned home from a trip in January 2001, after two years filled with weekend getaways, I decided enough was enough. I needed a break. It sounds bizarre, but I was starting to feel as though I were living two separate lives. It was both expensive and emotionally challenging to maintain them both. I decided to pull in the reins on Miami Michi and focus on advancing my career. My drive for professional success and my desire to maintain my role as a strong and grounded woman overpowered my secret desire to be a carefree beach diva. I also decided to go back to school. I had completed a two-year program at a community college a few years earlier, but I really wanted my bachelor's degree. I threw myself into work and school with a vengeance.

My break was short-lived. By May, I couldn't take it any longer: work was stressful, and I needed a break from the responsibility. I booked a trip for a four-day weekend in mid-June.

I spent the first three days relaxing on the beach, but on my last night in town, Janis and I decided it was time to let loose.

Janis worked at one of the hottest new restaurants, Touch, located on Lincoln Road, one of the pulsating streets that South Beach was famous for. We decided to start our evening there and then see where the night might take us.

We sat at the bar and Janis ordered one of her favorite drinks, an appletini. I'd never been a big drinker, but I didn't want to be a downer, so I ordered a rum and Coke to sip on. The bar was strategically placed in the center of the room, perfect for soaking in the scene. For the next half hour we took in the ambiance and live entertainment—a crazy show featuring belly dancers and fire-eaters. This dimly lit restaurant—the site for a Playboy shoot and countless celebrity dinners—was designed to entice all of the senses. As usual, I was mesmerized.

Finally, the hostess let us know that she had room for us on the upper deck. By the time we reached our table, Janis was laughing. "I think you broke the neck of every guy at the bar," she teased me. "Your skirt should be X-rated, girl."

Janis and me out in Miami

I smiled and lovingly responded, "Shut up!" as I elbowed her in the ribs. From the time I was fourteen, I'd known I had the kind of curves that attract attention. This was precisely why I preferred pantsuits and rarely wore skirts. I wanted to be seen and known for my mind and business skills. But whenever I was in Miami, that all flew out the window. After years of wearing mainly business attire, I felt liberated.

Our waiter appeared and gave Janis a big hug and the infamous South Beach kiss. Then he turned to me. "Hi, I'm Mark. I'll be taking care of you ladies this evening."

I immediately noticed his eyes: deep hazel with flecks of green and gold, and a mischievous glint. His black hair was set off by adorable reddish sideburns.

He picked up my empty glass. "What were you drinking?"

I quickly glanced at Janis. Luckily, she was more focused on the scene around us than on what I was drinking. "How about Coke on the rocks, but leave it in the glass with the little straw?" I said under my breath. "I want it to look like I am still drinking, if you know what I mean."

He chuckled. "All right. And another appletini for you, Janie-J?"

Janis nodded distractedly, and with that he was gone.

As Mark walked away, I took the opportunity to stare at him some more. He was solid muscle: six feet tall with big arms and broad shoulders. I couldn't help but notice he had an amazingly cute butt. I liked tall guys, but usually with light-colored hair and blue eyes. Mark wasn't my type, but he was yummy.

Janis caught me staring. "You like him, huh?"

"He's pretty cute," I said, trying to sound casual.

"I know, and really sweet. I think he's single. Want me to hook you up?"

I smiled and glanced over at him again. "No, I'm leaving in the morning. I'll probably never see him again. I'll just enjoy the view for the evening."

Mark returned with our drinks. "These are on the house, enjoy. The chef will be preparing something special to start, so no need to look at the menus."

"Thanks, babe," Janis said, smiling back.

The special attention was nice but didn't surprise me. The chef had a fancy for Janis. As she and I chatted, I found myself glancing over her shoulder to watch Mark as he maneuvered around the room. At each of his tables, he appeared to be fully engaged with his customers, even laughing with them. He had a distinctive laugh that filled the whole room.

"Are you listening to me? What are you staring at?" Janis asked.

"Nothing, nothing," I answered.

She turned her head and saw Mark standing at a table nearby. "You're watching him, aren't you?"

"No. Just go back to your story."

The food runner brought the first course, a tantalizing marinated beef strip salad on hearts of palm with balsamic dressing. Mark stopped to check on us and see what else we might need.

"By the way," he added, "there are some gentlemen at the bar who would like to buy you a drink. Shall we take them up on their offer?"

"Absolutely," Janis replied. Moments later he returned with the drinks. Before he could leave, Janis blurted out, "Michi, did you know Mark is from Knoxville?"

I knew she was trying to bait us into conversation, and it worked. "Really?" I asked. "My mom lives in Knoxville, off Clinton Highway and Raccoon Valley Road. Do you know the area?"

"Wow, small world," he said. "My mom lives off the other end of Raccoon Valley. When are you going home again?"

I paused. Since I had never lived with my mom, Knoxville really wasn't home to me. Then I figured, *Ah, what the hell.* "I don't know. When are you going home again?" I flashed him a flirtatious smile and batted my eyes.

"Soon. We'll have to coordinate a visit home after I check on my other tables. Be back shortly."

When he was out of sight, Janis and I burst into laughter. I was clearly flirting and he was clearly taking the bait.

The food and drinks kept flowing, and Janis and I continued enjoying our evening.

When Mark came to clear the dishes, he asked what I was doing the next day.

"Leaving town. I've got to get back to work."

"Too bad, I'm off tomorrow. Who's ready for dessert?"

Both of us were, and minutes later he set down a luscious chocolate mousse with two spoons. Janis scooped up a spoonful and turned to entice Mark with a taste. He bent down, fixed his eyes on mine, and opened his mouth. As Janis slid the spoon onto his tongue, his eyes rolled back and closed in ecstasy. I couldn't stop my imagination from conjuring up vivid thoughts of him in compromising positions. *I'm going to get into trouble with this one,* I thought as a smile spread across my face.

"Well, what are you all doing with the rest of your evening?" he asked as he straightened.

Again, I pondered my response. Before I'd set my eyes on him, I hadn't planned on anything other than heading home and packing for my early morning flight. Although it was late by normal standards, the night was still young in South Beach. "Well, that all depends," I said at last. "What time do you get off?"

"I should be out of here within thirty minutes."

"We'll see if I'm still at the bar when you're done. Better hurry."

Janis and I paid the tab and headed to the bar, found two empty stools, and planted ourselves while we waited for a few more friends to get off work.

"Wow, you're still here!" I heard someone say. I turned to find Mark standing behind me in his black dress slacks and an old, ratty used-to-be-white undershirt. His black dress shirt was slung over his shoulder, along with his tie. He looked amazing.

"That was the longest thirty minutes I've ever experienced," I said in a sarcastic tone. "More like an hour and a half, wouldn't you say?" I turned back toward the bar.

"Yeah, yeah, yeah. You're still here, aren't you?"

I grinned at him. "Well then, I guess this just happens to be your lucky night!"

He ordered a drink, and during the next half hour, I got the abbreviated version of how Mark had spent his early and mid twenties. A drifter, he had lived in Hawaii for two years, traveled the world with only a knapsack for a year and a half, and spent the rest of his time in beach communities throughout the United States. His astrological sign was Cancer, and he had a birthday coming up on June 30. He'd never had a serious girlfriend and never stayed anywhere too long. He gave me the impression he had chosen this nomadic lifestyle because it created opportunities for both new experiences and plenty of solitude. I found this extremely intriguing; it was the complete opposite of my structured, workaholic life.

Even though we were the same age, our lives up until that point had been vastly different. I had worked for the same company for nine years. I'd been married and divorced. Any free time I had was devoted to completing my bachelor's degree or to the gym. The only deviations from my predictable routine were my weekend getaways to Miami and the month Janis and I had spent in Africa two years earlier. Mark's carefree, transient life totally fascinated me.

"Are you guys ready?" Janis asked. "We're all heading to Cro-Bar."

Mark turned to me and said, "I'll meet you guys there. I need to go home and change."

I hesitated. I had no real interest in going to Cro-Bar. I was only interested in learning more about Mark.

"You aren't driving?" I asked him, wondering how he'd get home.

"No, I have my skateboard with me."

The image of this guy riding his skateboard to and from work made me smile, and I couldn't help but laugh. I hadn't seen a skateboard since I was maybe fourteen, and I couldn't wrap my brain around the idea of a grown man using one as his main mode of transportation. I suggested that I drive him in my rental car to get changed. He was quick to take me up on my offer.

I pulled up in front of his building, expecting Mark to jump out, run in, and change while I waited. "Park right there, I want to show you something," he said.

I parked and followed him to his high-rise. He led me to the back of the building. Just beyond the pool, I could see the reflection of the moon in the bay. At two a.m., it was beautiful, quiet, and peaceful. I knew he liked to travel, but I couldn't help but think that if I lived there, I'd never want to leave. Mark stood a few feet behind me as I stared at the water. Butterflies fluttered in my stomach as I wondered what would come next. Unexpectedly, he grabbed my upper arms, pulled me in close, and kissed me. *What was that?* I was caught off guard, but I also kind of liked it.

I nudged him to hurry up and get changed, and then followed him upstairs to his apartment. We walked past the small kitchen with outdated appliances into what appeared to be the living area. His furnishings consisted of an air mattress with a stack of books next to it, a stereo, an acoustic guitar,

Mark, the drifter in Hawaii

and two plastic lawn chairs. A frameless oil painting in vibrant colors was taped to the wall. As I glanced around the apartment, I thought of my own fully furnished and nicely decorated apartment, with its new appliances, granite countertops, and garden tub. It was instantly obvious that our living standards were as vastly different as our lifestyles, which made Mark even more intriguing.

He flipped the stereo on, and the music of Aaron Neville filled the room. He pulled me close and pressed his lips against my one cheek and then the other, and then each eyelid before kissing my lips. When he released me, he headed toward the closet and removed his shirt.

25

"You know I am not going to Cro-Bar, right?" he said.

"What?"

"My only interest in going to the club was to hang out with you. Now I have you all to myself, so I don't want to go to the club. I won't be able to hear you above the noise of the music. Besides, I'm alone with you here and I don't really fancy sharing you." He looked directly at me.

"I guess we could just hang here for a while," I said hesitantly. "I'm not going down there by myself."

"I'm glad that's settled. Come over here and sit with me?" He motioned to the air mattress.

We spent the next hour alternating between casual conversation and heavy make-out sessions. Eventually, Mark announced that he wanted to change out of his work slacks. As he went into the bathroom, I took the opportunity to slip out onto the patio to investigate the view. A million thoughts raced through my mind. I didn't want a one-night stand, but the intense attraction between us had knocked me off balance and clouded my head. How far did I want this to go? Did I tell him what I knew about HPV? Did I even have HPV? Didn't everyone have it? Wait, maybe he had HPV. I was so confused.

I was still lost in my own head when I felt Mark come up from behind me, put his arms around me, and kiss my neck. His soft kisses sent chills down my back. As I spun around, I saw that he had changed out of his work pants and into board shorts that showed off his toned physique. I took a deep breath. *You are in so much trouble, girl!*

"As cute and inviting as you are," I said, "let's get one thing straight: I'm not going to sleep with you tonight." I tried to say it like I meant it.

"That's fine. I respect that, but you can't blame a guy for trying, can you?"

"I suppose not."

It wasn't that I was such a good girl. Since my divorce almost two years earlier, I had dated a few guys; and when I had sex with them, I did so without considering the potential risk. But then, after that second gynecological scare, I had learned more about HPV. I didn't know if I actually had the virus or not, but I knew it was a likely culprit in my past health issues. If I did have it, I had no idea who had given it to me or how long ago. Why risk passing it on for just a one-night stand? Plus, I had been feeling more and more like I was ready for something meaningful. I didn't know exactly what that was, but I knew it wasn't another fly-by-night relationship.

We lay on his air mattress and talked, and I didn't realize how much time had passed until the first rays of sun started to light the sky. I didn't want to leave, but I had a flight to catch. Missing it was not an option. He grabbed a tie-dye sarong, wrapped it around his almost naked body, and slid his feet into a pair of black "slaps." Most people call them flip-flops but Mark had his own, unique slang that was as crazy as his Gypsy lifestyle.

As Mark walked me to my rental, he said, "So, if I happened to be in D.C. sometime, would you go to dinner with me?"

"I don't know if I know you well enough," I teased. "You'll just have to wait and see."

He leaned in to kiss me again, pressing me against the SUV. "I have never wanted anyone as bad as I want you right here, right now!"

I knew exactly what he meant. The chemistry between us was intense.

I called Janis on my cell phone as I drove to the airport. She didn't answer, so I recorded my apology for not showing up at the club and hung up. When the plane landed in D.C., I headed straight for work. I was ready to slip back into my usual busy routine: work, an hour a day at the gym, and class two nights a week as I worked toward a degree in organizational management.

I tried not to think about my chance encounter with Mark. Logic told me to forget him; he'd never call. But secretly, I hoped I was wrong about this guy. So when my phone rang not long after I got to work, I grabbed it and attempted to disguise my excitement.

It was Janis. "Well, sounds like someone had a good night."

"I guess you could say that," I said, trying not to make it seem like a big deal. I shared the details and joked about coming back down in two weeks for the Fourth of July. Janis loved visits from me, so of course she encouraged the idea. At first I wasn't sure, but the more I mulled over the thought, the better it sounded. The trip could serve two purposes: another weekend with Janis and another chance to see Mark. I toyed around with the idea all day and even checked the prices of plane fares when I got home that night.

The next day came and went uneventfully with no call from Mark. I wasn't surprised, but I was disappointed. The odds were that our one night together would be just that. This guy was so intriguing and so different from anyone I had ever dated, though. I thought maybe he would surprise me.

The following morning got off to a bumpy start. I accidentally turned off the alarm instead of hitting snooze and woke up an hour late. I raced around the house trying to get ready for work. When I finally made it out to the car, I realized I had forgotten my books for class. I rushed back into the house and spotted them by the computer. As I grabbed them, I noticed the printout with the airfares. Without hesitating, I logged on and, in just a few keystrokes, booked another ticket for paradise. *Even if I don't run into Mark, I'll still have a blast with Janis*, I told myself, trying to justify my impulsiveness.

Later that afternoon, I noticed a missed a call on my cell phone. I recognized the 305 area code as Miami and knew it was not Janis's number. Butterflies fluttered in my stomach.

I dialed my voice mail and heard: "Hey, Michi. I just wanted to make sure you got home safely and to say hello. Oh, by the way, this is Mark. Give me a call sometime."

He called! My heart raced with excitement. Did I call him back? Now? No, maybe it was better to wait until that night. I felt like a lovesick teenager.

Deciding it was time for my lunch break, I clocked out and headed toward the door. As soon as I was outside, my fingers were dialing Mark's number. I paced back and forth in front of the store as I listened to the phone ring and ring. My anxiety and anticipation grew with each second.

Finally he answered.

"Hey, how's it going?" I tried to play it cool, but my voice quivered.

"Great! It is nice to hear your voice, Michi."

We spent the next few minutes engrossed in small talk, sharing the details of all that had transpired in the hours since we had been together.

"So, how about that dinner?" Mark asked abruptly.

"Dinner? What? When?"

"In a month. I hope you'll allow me to take you out."

"Are you really going to come up here?"

"I've arranged a detour through D.C. on my way to visit my mom in Knoxville."

I told him I could pick him up at the airport, and then asked where he was staying. He confessed he didn't know anyone else in the area and he had no place to stay.

"Well then, you will stay with me. My couch will love the company!" I laughed. "Now that that's settled, I have some good news. I'm coming back to Miami!"

The best part was that my trip was barely two weeks away. We wouldn't have to wait a full month to see each other again.

I went back to work, but I had trouble staying focused for the rest of my shift, and an even harder time sitting through my class that evening. My thoughts bounced between memories of our evening together in Miami and every word of our last call. And then there were the questions: Do I ask about his past sexual experiences and health? Do I share mine? And if so, when? After class, I raced out and headed straight for the gym. I was full of energy. I knew I would never fall asleep without burning some of it off.

Me physically fit

Fireworks ─────────────────────

July 2001

Those two weeks flew by, and before I knew it I was back on a plane to Miami, my mind still full of questions.

What will it be like to see him again? Will the same chemistry still flow between us? What is the point of pursuing this when we live so far away from each other?

By the time the plane pulled up to the gate, I was filled with such excitement and anticipation, I practically sprang out of my seat. I went straight to Janis's apartment where I found her lounging in bed watching videos on MTV. We spent about twenty minutes catching up, until Janis said, "All right already! Are you gonna call him or what?"

It was the push I needed. I picked up my cell phone and dialed Mark's number.

"Hola, senorita," he answered. "Are you finally here? Where exactly are you?"

"I just got to Janis's place. I was wondering what you were up to."

"Just relaxing on the beach. Want to come down and join me?"

"Absolutely."

I threw on my favorite bright blue bikini and a pair of comfy gray cotton shorts, grabbed one of Janis's beach bags full of lotion, stuffed a towel into it, and headed for the door.

The beach was packed full of locals and tourists baking in the sun. I wondered if I'd ever find Mark, but then I saw a man with dark hair, wide shoulders, and a stack of books lying next to a skateboard. *There he is.*

He greeted me with a kiss. We sat and talked for a while, until Mark exclaimed that it was too hot and he needed to take a dip. We ran into the ocean.

We alternately dunked each other and kissed, until Mark said out of the blue, "I bought a bunch of flowers this morning and arranged a beautiful bouquet in a vase at my apartment."

"Oh." *What a random comment,* I thought.

"Would you like to check it out?" he asked.

"Sure, I'd be honored to see your creation." Now it was clear. The flowers were his ploy to get me from the very public beach back to his very private apartment.

Mark's apartment was exactly as I remembered, with only one exception: a small, round wooden table holding a clear vase full of beautiful flowers. The scent of the flowers—roses, daisies, lilies, and carnations—filled the space.

"They're beautiful," I said. "And real!"

"What do you mean?" Mark asked.

"I thought you made up the flowers just to lure me here."

"Come here, goofball," Mark said as he grabbed my hand and yanked me toward him. He gently kissed my forehead and hugged me tightly. He lit some incense. We lay down on the floor together and started talking. Words seemed to come so easily to me around him, which surprised me. I'm usually quiet and emotionally prudent, rarely letting others get beyond the surface. It was different with Mark. I didn't feel the need to hold anything back. We could talk about everything and nothing at all. Even moments of silence flowed effortlessly, which added to the peace I felt when I was with him.

In just our swimsuits, with the heat between us growing, it was hard to keep our hands off each other. Even when just chatting, our bodies seemed to reach for each other. First our feet would tangle. Then his foot would slide up my leg, and instantly we'd be in each other's arms. We explored each other's bodies, but I always pulled away before it escalated too far.

Finally, Mark had to get ready for work. I walked with him to the restaurant, and he said he'd call me once he finished. I knew it would be late and I wanted to wait up but by three, I was half-asleep and still hadn't heard from him. I recalled our afternoon together, and for an instant I felt silly for acting so carefree and open with him, like a teenage girl with an impractical crush. *Really, what could ever come of this relationship?*

Around 4:30 a.m., the phone rang.

"Hey, you. Are you still up?"

"Sort of. What's happening?"

"Swimming! Want to come with me?"

I responded without thinking. "Sure, I'll be over in a minute."

Suddenly, I felt energized. I grabbed a few things and rushed out the door. As I walked the ten blocks, feeling the gorgeous night air blowing across my face, I wondered why this guy was having such a strange effect on me. I was acting purely on impulse and loving every second of it.

His door was unlocked. I walked in and saw him lying on the air mattress. He pulled me down next to him and kissed me. *I guess we're not going swimming.*

That kiss started another round of cat and mouse between us. We kissed passionately while Mark attempted to get me out of my clothes. I craved his touch and wanted to give in, but my good sense kept chiming in and I'd pull back. Even though my marriage hadn't worked out, I remembered how great it was to share daily life with someone who interested me mentally, physically, and spiritually, and who challenged me to be a better version of myself. I wanted a relationship with depth, not a roll in the hay. I wasn't quite ready to admit this even to myself, but deep down I knew I missed marriage, stability, forever. Plus, I still hadn't initiated the talk about our previous sexual experiences and our health, and it weighed on my mind.

Our kissing and caressing escalated, though never as far as Mark wanted, until he abruptly pulled back. "I can't do this," he said. "I want you, but I'm not going to force you."

We sat in silence for a few minutes as I processed what he had said, the last few days, and my conflicting emotions. I realized I wasn't being fair. I knew what I wanted, and I didn't want to ruin the moment with an awkward conversation. I moved closer to him and kissed him.

"No," he said. "I can't keep doing this."

I kissed him again and again, until he kissed me back. "Take me," I whispered.

The sex was just as crazy and hot and amazing as I had fantasized it would be.

"Wow, Happy Fourth of July," Mark exclaimed just before I drifted off to sleep.

We spent the rest of my visit in bed talking, laughing and having mind-blowing sex. When we wanted a break, we strolled a few blocks to the movie theater to catch a flick, since Mark didn't own a TV.

The more time I spent with Mark, the more he captivated me. I was totally amazed by his sincerity. He said hello to strangers we passed on Ocean Drive and treated everyone with genuine kindness, from the crazy old lady walking her dog, to the homeless guy on the corner. When we went into a shop for a soda, he'd always ask the clerk how his shift was going, and he'd actually wait for a response before handing over his money.

Mark also had a spiritual curiosity that appealed to me. He had books about religion, philosophy, and self-discovery. I was in the midst of my own spiritual awakening and had started to question my ideas of God and religion.

My dad had raised my sisters and me loosely in line with his Christian views. I was baptized an Episcopalian, but we rarely went to church. However, one thing stuck with me: my dad always said that if two people prayed together in Jesus's name, the prayer had more power.

Just before I met Mark, I found myself wanting to reconnect with my spirituality. The two years of jetting back and forth between Maryland and Florida had been a way for me to get to know and understand sides of myself that I had repressed, but they had also left me feeling burned-out and exhausted. I needed a deeper sense of meaning in my life.

I started seeking out a broader understanding of religion and spirituality. I attended church with any friend that went. I tried many Christian denominations and took classes that explored some Eastern religions. I even went to a few temples and mosques, taking wisdom and truths from each one, but not feeling at home anywhere.

Then in March 2001 I decided to return to the Episcopal church where I had been baptized. It seemed to fit me—all of me. My disciplined, responsible side loved the ritual and structure of the service. The rest of me loved the openness of the Episcopal faith: women were priests, no one cared about the church leaders' sexual orientation, and even divorce was accepted as a part of life. I finally found a spiritual home, and I started to find answers to some of my larger existential questions. The more I allowed myself to open up to this new faith, the more at peace I felt. I approached people and experiences with a more open heart and mind. Instead of trying to control my world so tightly, I started asking, "What am I supposed to learn from this experience or person?"

I brought this new sense of openness to my budding romance. So, while a lot of what was happening with Mark didn't seem practical, a part of me felt that it was all happening for a reason. For once I was willing to let go and see where it would lead.

Feminine Itch

July 2001

Being with Mark gave me a natural high that I was still riding two days after I left Miami. Unfortunately, it was just enough time for the irritation and intense itching in my vaginal area to set in.

I wish this had come as a surprise, but it didn't. I was more prone to yeast infections than anyone I knew. The first one had struck in my early twenties, and from then on it seemed like almost anything would bring about an unwelcome visit. The usual suspects were things like wearing my jeans too tight or having sex after months of celibacy, but sometimes it felt like even breathing the wrong way brought about another infection.

It's a totally normal, totally annoying part of being female. Almost every woman I know has gotten at least one in her lifetime. I nicknamed it "baking bread." It made my friends laugh and made an uncomfortable subject easier to talk about. Most of my friends were afraid to discuss this part of their health, even with their gynecologists. They would rather get some over-the-counter drug from the drugstore, deal with it at home, and pretend it never happened.

On the one hand, I get it. The itching, burning, and scratching, accompanied by that wonderful discharge, do not make for great dinner conversation. On the other hand, I think that part of the reason sexual health is so taboo is that when anything goes wrong "down there," it is perceived as dirty. Not talking about it just perpetuates this stigma. In my case, I was getting these infections so often I couldn't avoid talking about it. That may have saved my life.

The frequent infections meant that Dr. T. and I had gotten to know each other very well over the years. Sometimes I felt like I was living at the gynecologist's office. It seemed like once a month I was either calling for an appointment or asking for a prescription. Given the sexually active weekend with Mark, I was pretty sure I knew the cause of my latest discomfort. I called the nurse's hotline and explained my situation.

"No, I really don't think it is necessary to see the doctor," I said as the

Nurse tried to schedule an appointment. "If it doesn't clear up after taking the Diflucan, I'll call back."

Sure enough, I took the medicine, and within forty-eight hours I was feeling better.

Two weeks later Mark came to visit me. Once again, we spent all of our time learning more about each other, eating, being intimate, and relaxing in front of the big screen at the local cinema. When the weekend was over, he boarded a plane for Knoxville to visit his mother, and I returned to work and school. I didn't have any immediate signs of another infection, so I thought I was in the clear.

About a week later, I realized something wasn't right. After work, I went straight home to take a bath. I was itching and burning so badly, I thought I was going to scream. I'd always been a believer that women should do visual checks of not just their breasts, but also of their lady lips. So I got a mirror and checked out my girl parts. I was surprised to see a red rash.

This is new! My mind started to race. *What if he's given me a STD?*

I grabbed the cordless phone and dialed the nurse's hotline as I sank into the tub. "I need to make an appointment with Dr. T.," I told the nurse. Of course, they always want all the embarrassing details, so I gave them to her. I was lucky: there was one appointment with Dr. T. first thing in the morning. The itching was feeling more like pain now, and my fear and anxiety were growing. I didn't think I'd last until morning. I grabbed some Monistat external cream and applied it after the bath, and then wrapped an ice pack in a soft towel and placed it between my legs. *What was happening to me?*

I barely slept a wink, worrying all night about the STD I might have. I rose early and dressed for the appointment, wearing just loose-fitting sweatpants and a T-shirt.

The nurse took all the usual information and then handed me the standard-issue white gown. I slipped off my pants and took my position on the table. Dr. T. entered minutes later.

"Please tell me I don't have an STD," I said.

"Slow down. Tell me what's going on and then I'll take a look."

After I explained my symptoms, she performed an examination and took cultures. When she was done, she told me to get dressed while she looked at cultures under a microscope. She returned quickly and said that I had a very bad yeast infection.

"What about the rash?" I asked, puzzled.

"Yeast naturally lives in the vagina, and a yeast infection is merely an overgrowth of this yeast. However, sometimes when the overgrowth of yeast is very high, a rash can be one symptom. You get these infections frequently, and this is the worst one yet. Keep an eye on it, and if it doesn't get better in a week or so, come back and see me."

I did just as Dr. T, instructed, and the infection went away. I was definitely relieved. It was the worst case of "baking bread" I'd ever encountered, which was saying a lot. I was so relieved not to have a STD that I happily put the whole experience behind me. What I didn't realize then was that this was more than just another annoying infection. It was a warning sign of things to come.

Magic Words

August 2001

Mark had visited me in late July. Only a week later, I missed him terribly and wanted more time with him. I had plenty of vacation time saved and couldn't think of a better way to spend it than in South Beach. I purchased a ticket for early August.

The night before I left for Miami, during one of our now daily phone conversations, Mark asked where I was staying.

"With Janis. Where else?"

"I was hoping you'd stay with me."

"Are you sure?" I asked.

"Yes. I'd love to have you."

"Okay. I'll come straight to your place."

The next day, I arrived at Mark's apartment just after 2:00 p.m. The door was unlocked, and I found Mark still snuggled up on his air mattress. It had been only three weeks since we'd seen each other, but it felt like months. We instantly formed a human pretzel; our bodies wrapped and intertwined until we were one. After a short nap, we had just enough time to take a quick dip in the pool before Mark headed off to work.

I sat at the bar sipping a glass of wine and watching the scene while both Mark and Janis worked that night. They got off work around one a.m. A bunch of their coworkers were planning on heading to Cro-Bar and asked us join them. Mark declined, so I did as well.

Outside he hailed a cab and gave the driver an address I didn't recognize. I looked at him quizzically. Mark smiled and said, "We're house-sitting tonight, silly."

The cab dropped us off outside a small yellow bungalow in a neighborhood I didn't recognize. Mark grabbed my hand and led me inside. Once the door closed behind us, he stripped down and ran to the back of the house. I heard a loud splash and poked my head through the blinds. The backyard was small, surrounded by a six-foot concrete wall, and a large pool filled the entire space.

I hesitated for a moment and then threw off my clothes and joined him under the starlit sky for a swim. The change in environment was fun and exciting, and it sparked a heightened sense of adventure in me.

The next day, while we were watching TV, a girlfriend from home called to tell me about a dream she'd had the night before. In her dream, Mark and I ran off and got married. I laughed. Mark asked about the call after I hung up. Thinking he, too, would find it funny, I told him.

Big mistake.

He sat up and with a stern look announced, "I'm moving to Taiwan when the season's over."

"Okay, why are you telling me this now?"

"I just want to be upfront, so you won't be upset when I leave."

"When is the season over?"

"January."

"Thanks for sharing," I mumbled, unable to hide my disappointment. "Don't you think you're jumping the gun just a bit? I don't even know if I'm still going to like you in January."

"What?" he said visibly shocked.

"Look, I like you, and I love spending time with you, but I live hundreds of miles away from you. I like things the way they are, in this moment. I just want to enjoy you and see what happens. But if you already have this all planned out, if you know how and when it's going to end, then there's no need to even continue." I stood up and walked out of the room.

Mark followed. "You're fine not having a commitment from me?"

I looked him directly in the eye. "Are you sleeping with anyone else?"

"No. Are you?" It was clear he was disturbed at the thought.

"No!"

We stood there, eyes locked, each waiting for the other person to say something.

I finally broke the silence. "Let's leave our relationship the way it is today. I want to be with you, and you want to be with me. If you change your mind or become interested in someone else, let me know. If you sleep with someone else, I deserve to know so I can decide if I still want to be involved with you. I'll do the same. Deal?"

"Deal." He looked at me for a moment and then said, "I've never seen a woman react like you. Everyone I've dated in the past wanted a promise or some sort of guarantee, and it always got messy in the end. I just wanted to avoid that."

I laughed. "You'll learn that I'm not every other woman you've been with. Anyway, I may be tired of you by then!"

Mark and me heading out for dinner   Mark and me goofing off at Touch

The rest of our time together was pure bliss. During the day I'd laze around with Mark or meet up with Janis at the beach, where we would work on our tans. On the nights when Janis and Mark worked, I passed the time by watching the eclectic parade of people on the street, reading a book, or seeing a movie, eventually making my way down to meet them at the bar. On nights he didn't work, Mark would pick a nice restaurant and take me to dinner, where we would share a bottle or two of wine as he attempted to expand my palate. Every night we started with grand plans of dinner, a jazz club and dancing, but after a few glasses of wine, we always found ourselves back at his place, lost in each other.

Although we spent most of his free time together, we also gave each other space to come and go as we each pleased. There was no pressure, expectations, or obligations. We just flowed.

I had an evening flight back home, and neither Mark nor I wanted to get up and face our last day together. We slept in, staying snuggled on his air mattress until the early afternoon. Finally Mark couldn't ignore his growling stomach and ordered takeout. We ate in bed with the sliding door open, letting the salty ocean air fill the room. I wanted to freeze time, but I knew that was impossible. Reluctantly, I started getting ready to leave. While I packed, Mark stayed out on his balcony talking on the phone. When I finished packing, I joined him out there.

"Should I call a cab for you?" he asked.

"Unfortunately, it is that time," I said.

He called a local taxi service. The cab would be there in five minutes, so he suggested we wait downstairs."

We stepped into the elevator and rode in silence to the lobby. Neither of us looked at the other. This was the first time I felt uncomfortable. *What was going on?* I wondered. *He was so distant.*

Outside he put his arms around me and held me until the cab pulled up. The driver placed my suitcase in the trunk, and Mark opened my door.

"I'll call when I get home," I said.

Mark kissed me, looked me in the eyes, and said, "I love you, Michi." *What? You what? No, he didn't just say what I thought I heard.*

Stunned, I just stared at him. He nudged me into the cab, closed the door, and waved good-bye. "He loves me," I said out loud as tears rolled down my cheeks. *Wow!*

I was falling in love, too, but I also knew he had no intention of sticking around. He had made it clear he was heading to Taiwan at the end of the season. I was confused. Part of me wanted to scream at the top of my lungs that I loved him too, but I needed to keep this situation in perspective. I wanted to enjoy him now and then be able to let him go when the time came.

The next time we spoke, Mark ended the call with those magic words: "I love you, baby."

"I love you too, Mark," I said.

We spoke every couple of days, Mark usually called when he got off work and woke me up. He claimed he loved hearing my sleepy voice, and I didn't mind.

During the day, I focused on working and completing my degree. Every three or four weeks, one of us would take a flight so we could spend a weekend together. Since Miami Michi was dying to get out, I usually went to him. I loved leaving my everyday grind behind, escaping to South Beach and into Mark's waiting arms. The weekends were all the same. We secluded ourselves in his apartment every minute that he wasn't working, leaving only to grab food or to stroll down to the local movie theater.

It all felt so perfect.

Trouble on the Horizon————————————————

October to November 2001

As much as I loved going to see him, in October, Mark insisted on coming to Maryland to visit me. Fall was his favorite season; he loved watching the leaves turn colors and the smell of wood burning in fireplaces. It was also our first visit since the tragedy of 9/11. With all the heightened security causing headaches in airports across the country, I was relieved he was the one getting on a plane.

As excited as I was for him to see my home, I wasn't sure what we would do. My life in Maryland was consumed with exactly three things: work, school, and the gym.

Since Mark liked plays, I researched shows in the area. *The Vagina Monologues* was in town and sounded interesting. The show was supposed to be funny and had received rave reviews. More, I was curious to hear the down-and-dirty details of womanhood, no holds barred. I believed in the importance of being open, but I was only comfortable talking about my sexuality with my closest girlfriends.

It was also a bit of a test. Mark was open and easygoing, and I thought he would welcome the chance to try something new. I wanted to see if I knew him as well as I thought I did.

The show was amazing. I was inspired by the passion, raw honesty, and awareness that the play revealed out about the female experience. It made me wish more people were so open and comfortable talking about their "private" parts. Mark was clearly moved. The show brought up issues he had never thought about before, and he developed a new respect for some of the things women had to go through. He couldn't help but think he was lucky to be a man. I couldn't help but think he had passed the test with flying colors.

Two days after Mark left, I woke with an ache in my right breast. I looked in the mirror and noticed a red mark under my nipple. It was sensitive and warm to my touch. As the day wore on, the ache grew into an intense pain. I tried to ignore it, thinking I must have slept on it funny. My friend Andi's mom is a nurse, and when I asked her about it, she advised that I call

41

my doctor. By late afternoon, the red spot had grown in size and radiated a tremendous heat.

Alarmed, I called the nurses' hotline again. I didn't realize at the time that this phone call would change the entire course of my life.

Dr. T. could see me the next day, October 11, 2001. In the examining room, the nurse instructed me to undress from the waist up and slip on a paper shirt with the opening in the front. *This was different,* I thought. *Usually I was undressing from the waist down.*

When Dr. T. came in, I told her about my breast, and she inspected the area. She explained that my mammary gland was infected and I needed an antibiotic. She asked how things below were going. I told her I was continuing to get regular yeast infections and I was experiencing some pain after sex.

"I'd like to do an exam, if you don't mind," she said.

"No problem," I replied.

She left the room while I undressed. When she returned, I assumed the position. The usual drill. I stared at the plain white ceiling for what seemed like the hundredth time. *Couldn't they at least paint an interesting mural or something up there? Anything to take my mind off all that was happening down below.*

Dr. T. reported that my vagina was red and swollen, but things looked fine otherwise. She was going to do a culture just to be sure, and that I needed to come back in a few weeks. Once I was dressed, she wrote a few prescriptions and gave me instructions before sending me on my way.

I returned on October 25 for my follow-up. Dr. T. examined my breast and informed me that the infection had cleared up. Also, the vaginal cultures were negative. I told her I was still irritated down below.

"When was your last Pap?" she asked.

"About six months ago, in March, I believe."

"Let's perform another Pap test today. You shouldn't be experiencing such frequent yeast infections. Maybe something else is going on with you. It could be a sign of a weakened immune system."

About a week later, I received a call from the nurse. She told me the results were normal. That was a relief, but then she added, "Oh, Dr. T. requested a HPV DNA test on the cervical sample she took for your Pap test. It was positive."

"What?" I asked. What I was really thinking was, *Positive for what?*

"We have a new tool available called the human papillomavirus DNA test. While a traditional Pap test looks for abnormal cells usually caused by HPV, this test actually detects certain strains of the virus itself. In your case, it means you tested positive for high-risk HPV."

Much later, I would learn that certain strains of high-risk HPV can cause cancer. Sometimes the body fights them off. If it doesn't, the virus causes those cells to mutate and turn malignant. Not everyone with high-risk HPV will get cervical cancer, but it's definitely a red flag. Of course, the nurse did not explain all of that. She was just there to give me the results.

"What does that mean to me?" I asked.

"Well, in your case, probably nothing. Some of your past problems with abnormal cells were most likely caused by the presence of the HPV virus. But your Pap test was normal and you aren't experiencing any visible signs, so I wouldn't worry. I'll double-check with the doctor and let you know."

I hung up and thought about what she had just told me. *I have HPV. I actually have it. What does that really mean? And what exactly am I suppose to do with this knowledge? Do I tell Mark? Does he now have it?*

Dr. T. had never told me that HPV was definitely the cause of my past dysplasia, just that it was a possible cause. I was confused, but figured that if I had anything to worry about, I would hear from the doctor. I also decided not to mention the details of the HPV to Mark. I thought it would just make things weird. Plus, he had already slept with me, so it wasn't like he could undo that act. I pushed it out of my thoughts. Things were good with Mark, and I wanted to focus on that.

The day after Thanksgiving, Black Friday, is the busiest shopping day of the year, and therefore the busiest day for those of us who work in retail. I planned to spend the week before Thanksgiving in Miami with Mark and Janis. I would return home early Friday morning.

A few weeks had passed since I had talked to the nurse. She had said she would talk to the doctor and get back to me. On the one hand, I was anxious to hear that everything was okay. On the other, I figured no news was probably good news. I told myself that everything must be fine.

The day I was due to fly to Miami, I was going to work first and then leaving from there. I carefully chose an outfit with dual purpose in mind: professional for during the day and sexy for evening playtime in South Beach. It was a fitted black pantsuit with a conservative jacket that I would leave buttoned during the day. At night in South Beach, I would lose the jacket and reveal a baby-blue satin bustier that laced up the front.

When I arrived in Miami, I dumped my stuff in Mark's apartment, refreshed my makeup, and took off the jacket. I looked into the mirror. *Perfect!*

I walked the few short blocks to the restaurant, where Janis was perched at the hostess stand. She greeted me with a big hug and a kiss on the cheek. The place was packed, but I decided to try to find Mark for a quick hello. Almost a month had passed since we were last together, and I just wanted to see his face. I spotted him up a small flight of stairs with his back to me, serving a guest. I approached from behind and positioned myself against the railing so he'd walk right into me as he turned to leave the table. He did exactly as I planned, bumping into me with his hands full.

"Oh, excuse me," he said without looking up.

"No problem, handsome," I said.

His head rose as he recognized the voice. "Wow, baby, you look great!" He kissed me and then headed for the kitchen. I went to the bar and ordered a glass of wine, which I nursed for the rest of the evening.

Eventually, Mark finished his shift, and we quickly walked the several blocks to his high-rise, and then rushed into the apartment.

The next day, Monday, we got up before noon and headed to the beach with towels, water, and our current reading selections. As we were settling in, Mark asked if I'd heard from the doctor. When I said I hadn't, he suggested I call the nurse. As much as I was content to be blissfully ignorant, I knew he was right. I grabbed my cell phone and dialed the office. I explained to the nurse why I was calling, and she placed me on hold for several minutes. Finally, she returned to the phone. I could hear pages rustling as she apparently flipped through my chart.

"Oh, yes," she said finally. "Dr. T. does want to see you again to do a colposcopy. Can you come in this week?"

I had had colposcopies during all of that abnormal cell business when I was seventeen and again at age twenty-five. All I remembered was that it entailed a more detailed examination of the entire vagina. Still, it didn't sound good. "No, I'm not in town. What's available next week?"

"How about the thirtieth at two p.m.?" she asked.

"Perfect."

"Okay, remember not to douche, use vaginal creams, or have sexual intercourse for forty-eight hours prior to your appointment. Also, it helps to take Advil or Tylenol first, in case the doctor needs to take biopsies. It will ease the cramping. We'll see you next week."

She hung up, and I sat there digesting the information for a minute.

"What did she say?" Mark asked.

I hesitated. I wasn't sure exactly how much of my medical history to share. Plus, I didn't even know what it all meant.

"She wants to schedule a colposcopy."

"Sounds kind of scary. What is it?"

I told him the little I knew. "It's a procedure that allows the doctor to more closely examine my vagina, cervix, and vulva. I'm not sure exactly what she's looking for, but I guess we'll find out."

Like a lot of guys, Mark was ignorant about the inner workings of female anatomy, so while he was teaching me about the world, I was teaching him about the vagina. Maybe it should have been weird, since this was such a new relationship, talking about my personal medical business, but Mark seemed interested. He asked lots of questions and actually listened to the answers. I never felt judged by him.

I had told Mark earlier that the lease on my apartment was up in December, and late that day he surprised me by remembering that. He asked about my plans, and I told him I truly didn't know. I was ready for a change, but I hadn't decided what that would look like. I hoped more might come of our relationship, but I knew it was unlikely, given Mark's carefree, pick-up-and-move-wherever-the-wind-blows lifestyle. Then he said he was considering staying in the States when the season was over instead of going to Taiwan. I was shocked. Just a few months before, he had been so adamant about not getting attached. I tried to play it cool, but I couldn't resist the urge to dig and find out what had changed his mind. He said he was thinking of going to Memphis. His brother was attending law school there, and he figured if he was going to stay in the States for a while longer, he'd like to be near family.

Where does that leave me … us? I was too afraid to ask.

The day after Thanksgiving, I rose early, kissed Mark good-bye, and headed to the airport. Work was waiting, and for once I almost looked forward to being back home. The uncertainty about our relationship and my growing love for him made me feel vulnerable, and I didn't like it. I could only go with the flow for so long.

November 30 arrived, and I asked my younger sister, Lori, to accompany me to see the doctor. Lori and I are only eighteen months apart in age, but worlds apart in every other way. She's emotional and impulsive; she rarely holds a job for long and often relies on other people to take care of her, especially me. Even though she drives me crazy, I love her.

When we arrived at the doctor's, the receptionist told me that an emergency had come up and Dr. T. was unable able to see me. Instead, her partner, Dr. G., would perform the colposcopy. I didn't know it then, but that little switch would save my life. The nurse directed us to exam room four and there it was again—the dreaded blue chair. By this time, I knew the procedure. I got undressed and assumed the position. Lori amused herself by opening all the cabinet doors.

"Stop it and have a seat!" I snapped.

She didn't mind me and kept snooping until she heard the doctor tap on the door.

The door opened, and Dr. G. entered the room. He greeted us, his eyes were warm and compassionate. I liked him immediately.

"Are you ready to get started?" he asked.

My baby sister, Lori and me

"Let's get it over with."

He inserted the speculum and applied a cold solution to my cervix. Then he used the colposcope to examine the entire area. "Looks good down here," he said. "I don't see anything to biopsy today. Hang in there. I'll be done in just a minute." I took a deep breath and waited for him to finish. Then I heard, "Since you're here, let's just go ahead and do an ECC. It'll only take another minute."

"A what?" I asked.

"Take a deep breath. It's called an endocervical curettage, or an ECC for short. Basically, I'm inserting an instrument into the cervical canal. I'll scrape the sides and collect cell samples. It's sort of like a Pap, but instead of taking samples of the outside surface of the cervix where there are squamous—skin—cells, we'll test the inside of the cervical canal where you have glandular cells."

"Okay, if you think we need it," I said.

The whole thing only took a few seconds, but my stomach cramped and those seconds seemed like minutes. When he was done, he left the room so I could dress. When he returned, he told me I'd hear something in about a week or so, and he advised that I take Advil for the cramps. The usual instructions.

I headed straight home, thinking about nothing more than how excited I was to take a nap.

The Breakup

December 2001

While I was being inspected at the doctor's office on Friday, Mark was on his way to Gainesville, Florida to take in a football game and enjoy a weekend of fun with his brother and the guys from back home. We didn't talk the entire time he was gone. Monday morning he called just to say hi. Our conversation was short, and he seemed distant. I didn't know why, but I wasn't worried. I chalked it up to the fact that he and his friends had probably drunk too much, stayed up late, and had little to no sleep.

Mark was planning on coming to Maryland for Christmas but hadn't bought his ticket yet, so the next day I went home during lunch to research ticket prices online. I called him, excited to share my findings and plan our next visit.

Instead, I got blindsided. "Michi, I just can't do this anymore," he said.

"Do what?"

"The distance. I'd like to be friends, and if you'll still let me spend Christmas with you, I'd like to do that too."

"Hold on, wait a minute here." I was shocked, hurt. "Out of the blue you tell me that you want to be just friends. You're breaking up with me but you want to come for Christmas?" I tried to wrap my brain around what he had just told me. "That's the craziest thing I've ever heard."

I attempted to find out what was really behind his sudden change of heart, but couldn't get much out of him. He told me only that he was moving to Memphis after New Year's. My head was spinning and I wanted to burst into tears, but I needed to get back to work.

The rest of the day was agony. I replayed the conversation over and over in my head. *What the hell had happened with his friends?* I wondered. *He had been fine and then … What had they said to him? Did it have anything to do with my doctor's appointment? Had my health problems scared him off?*

I tried calling him later, but he had already left for work. Around three the next morning, I awoke to the phone ringing. Mark was on the line. He sounded like he was crying, which confused me even more. He was the one breaking up with me. What did he have to cry about?

"Mark, what is going on?"

"I love you so much, probably more than I've ever loved anyone. You're so special to me and I can't imagine not having you in my life."

For a moment, I thought he had changed his mind. The queasy feeling in the pit of my stomach almost subsided. His next words hit like a ton of bricks.

"I'll understand if you hate me for this and never speak to me again, but I hope we can still be friends."

I tried to hold back, but it was no use: tears streamed down my cheeks. "Tell me you don't love me, and I'll hang up and never bother you again!"

"I can't. I do love you, more than anyone."

"No, you don't get to do this. You can't call, tell me how much you love me, and then break up with me. Either you love me and we figure this out together, or you don't and it's over. You can't have it both ways."

My emotional temperature was rising as my feelings switched from disbelief to sadness and finally to anger. What the hell kind of a breakup was this? Was he telling me he loved me in the hopes it would make me feel better about him dumping me? If that was his plan, it wasn't working. In fact, I was more confused and frustrated than before. Then it came to me—he was scared, scared of his emotions, scared of getting hurt, scared of being vulnerable, as I was.

I calmed down and explained my thoughts to him, hoping he could acknowledge his own fears and doubts. I suggested that I move to Memphis, too, so we could live in the same city and give our relationship a real shot. The truth was, I was dying for change. I had lived in the same area all my life. I had worked at the same job for nine years. I had been thinking about relocating for a while. I had even put a down payment on a house in Boca Raton, Florida two years before I met Mark, but had gotten cold feet and backed out of the sale. At the time, it felt too impulsive, but things were different now. I was more open to taking risks, and I didn't feel like I had to have everything figured out. I ended the call cautiously optimistic.

The next day Mark called to say he had reconsidered and was back to wanting to part ways. He explained that moving frequently and saying good-byes was hard sometimes, but it was part of his way of life. He had few responsibilities and he liked it that way. Asking another person to make such a big sacrifice just to be with him was a level of commitment he wasn't ready to take on.

From his perspective, I had too much to give up: a career, a furnished apartment, friends, and school. He offered no guarantees, no safety net. I heard everything he said and knew he was right. I even appreciated his sincerity and honesty, and I knew I wasn't the only one hurting. In fact, hearing the pain in his voice, I suspected this breakup was harder on him. He had never dealt with these types of emotions before—wanting someone so much, but knowing and accepting his limitations. I had been married and knew that love alone couldn't make a relationship work. I also knew how painful it was to have to admit that and walk away.

I explained to him that he was not responsible for my decisions or actions. He didn't owe me anything other than the truth. I wanted change. I wanted to move. I had just been waiting for a reason. And I wasn't suggesting that we live together, only that we live in the same city. I wanted us to date like any normal couple, to see each other at our leisure without planning flights and making elaborate arrangements, and see how things went.

Days went by with no word. I went ahead and made plans to vacate my apartment at the end of the month. I would put most of my belongings in storage until I figured things out, and stay with my sister Lori for a month or so.

Almost a week after Mark had first hit me with the breakup news, the phone rang again in the middle of the night. I wasn't sleeping very well—I hadn't had a good night's sleep all week—so I grabbed it after the first ring. It was Mark, and this time I knew for sure he was crying.

"Are you serious about moving and giving us a try?" he asked.

"Yes, of course!"

"Okay, let's do it."

Relief flooded my body. We agreed that we were both adults, that we were responsible only for our own actions and choices, and that the one thing we owed each other was the truth.

I could hardly believe it: we were moving to Memphis!

Results

December 2001

I arrived at my office on Monday, December 10, excited to tell my boss about the pending move. I asked him to check into the possibility of a transfer. He worked quickly, calling me back before the day was over with the name of the district manager for Memphis area stores. Things were moving fast, and without a hitch so far.

I realized suddenly that almost two weeks had passed with no word from my doctor. I had been on such an emotional roller coaster, I had almost forgotten about my last examination. Why had no one called me with the results? I called my doctor's office, and after the usual long wait, a nurse finally got on the phone. I explained I was calling for results, and she put me on hold. When she returned, she requested a phone number for the doctor to call me back.

What the hell is going on? My panic started to rise. I'd been dealing with nurses since I was seventeen. I knew that if everything was normal, she would have given me the results herself.

Within the hour, Dr. G. was on the phone. He didn't give me much in the way of details. "We're going to need a larger sample. It will be best if we perform it under general anesthesia for your comfort. Are you available Wednesday morning?"

"Wednesday? You mean like the day after tomorrow?" I had belonged to this HMO nearly my entire life, and in my experience they didn't clear an operating room that fast. *This is not good.*

"Yes, Wednesday the twelfth at 8:00 a.m. You'll need to be there at 6:00. I'll have the nurse call you with all the information to get you preregistered. Have someone drive you."

Early Wednesday morning, Lori and I arrived at the same Catholic hospital where I was born. After a short wait, I was called back for pre-op. The nurse instructed Lori to remain in the waiting room and then led me to a hospital bed surrounded by a white curtain. On the bed was a gown, socks with treads on the bottom, a hair net, and a clear plastic bag. The nurse left me, pulling the curtain closed behind her. I took off my clothes and placed them in the bag. Then, one by one, I picked up the items from the bed and put them on.

Damn, hospitals are always so cold. I hate being cold. I climbed onto the bed and pulled the covers up to get warm.

When the nurse returned, she asked a few questions to verify my identity and to make sure I understood the scheduled procedure. She asked me to sign some documents and then set up an IV in my arm. On her way out, she put my chart on a tray on the other side of the curtain. When I was sure she was gone, I slid off the bed and tiptoed to the curtain's edge. I peeked out to be sure no one was looking and then grabbed the chart. *It was my chart,* I thought. *Everything written on it was about me, so why did I feel the need to be so sneaky?*

I knew there was something they weren't telling me, so I started flipping through the pages, eager to figure out what had my doctor so concerned. I wasn't exactly sure what I was looking for, but I figured I would know when I found it. I found the sheet that verified my procedure for that day, and skimmed all the medical words that meant nothing to me until I suddenly stopped. "Suspicious … malignancy. Comments: this case is being sent to the Armed Forces Institute of Pathology for their opinion."

Panic hit me like a tidal wave, and I dropped the chart on the bed.

Suspicious. Malignancy. Pathology. Though the words raced through my mind, I couldn't process their meaning. I wanted to scream, but a gut-wrenching fear paralyzed me. My brain felt like an electric radio that someone had just thrown into the bathtub and short-circuited. *I need help.*

Just then, a nun walked past my curtain. "Sister!" I yelled.

She stopped and poked her head in. "Yes, my child?"

"Please get my sister, Lori, from the waiting room."

Time stood still while I waited for the nun to return with Lori. *Suspicious. Malignancy.* I knew the meaning of those words, but my mind was so cloudy. I couldn't process or comprehend them.

Lori finally pushed through the curtain. "How are you?"

I didn't bother answering her. Instead I asked, "Malignant, what does it mean?"

The blood drained from her face. She swallowed. "Why?"

I picked up the chart, still opened to the page, and shoved it in her direction. Her face told me everything I needed to know.

She read it out loud: "'Suspicious for low endometrial or high endocervical malignancy.'"

Hearing her speak the words made them register more clearly for me. I was out of the fog now. Lori looked up but didn't say a word. Her eyes overflowed with tears. In that instant, we both knew that the doctors thought I had cancer.

Lori's gaze was full of fear. I was always the strong one, the responsible one who took care of everyone else. In the years since our dad had died, Lori had looked to me even more as a parental figure. She leaned on me and I let her. Her expression reminded me that no matter what, I was still the big sister and I needed to stay calm. I took a deep breath and pushed back my own fear.

"I'm going to be fine, Lori, fine," I said as I reached for her hand.

Dr. G. entered my cubicle, followed by a shorter, round man with beady eyes. Both wore scrubs. "How's the patient?" Dr. G. asked.

"Okay," I lied.

He casually introduced Dr. A., the gynecologic oncologist, as if it were a mere coincidence that he was present. Dr. G. reminded me that Dr. A. had examined me once before. I vaguely recalled the visit to his office. I hadn't thought there was anything to worry about when I had originally met him. Now, I was starting to connect the dots. I knew I had HPV and apparently the doctors suspected I had cancer. *Had all those yeast infections over the years been a warning sign?* I wondered.

Dr. G. explained briefly why I was at the hospital. "It's probably nothing, but we want to take a larger sample to examine more closely. Better safe than sorry."

Dr. A. spoke up and provided a more detailed description of the procedure. They planned to remove a cone-shaped piece of tissue, beginning at the base of my cervix and extending up into the middle of my cervical canal. Hence its name: cone biopsy.

I sat in silence as they delivered their prepared pre-op dialogue. They informed me of the possible risks, including infection and an incompetent cervix, a condition in which the cervix isn't strong enough to hold the uterus shut during pregnancy.

They finished their spiel and still no mention of the *C* word. I decided to go for it myself. "You think I have cancer," I said. "Isn't that why we are really here?"

They both seemed caught off guard by my question, and then Dr. A. tried to reassure me. "No one is saying you have cancer. We just want to look, explore a bit more to be sure everything is fine. Anyway, you are really too young to have cervical cancer. The average age of a cervical cancer patient is fifty. You're only twenty-six."

I wasn't convinced, but their words seemed to calm Lori. I was glad she looked better, but I knew in my gut that something was wrong.

After the doctors left to prep for the surgery, the anesthesiologist came in. He inserted a syringe into the IV line, and the next thing I knew, I was waking up disoriented and in a lot of pain. After the pain stabilized, I was moved to a recovery room where the nurses focused on getting me to drink, eat a bag of crackers, keep the food down, and finally pee.

Dr. G. came by to see me for a minute. He explained that they hadn't performed the cone biopsy after all. Once my cervix had been dilated, they had seen the bottom edge of a growth inside my cervical canal and had used a laser to remove a sample to biopsy. He reviewed the post-op care with me: no sex, no bathtubs, no creams in the vagina for two weeks, Advil for pain, and plenty of rest. He assured me that I'd hear from him or Dr. A. in about a week.

I won't hold my breath, I thought. *You haven't called me back on time since this nightmare began!*

As Lori drove me home, I thought about what the doctors had said. I already knew in my core what the test would reveal. I glanced out the window and then at Lori. "I don't need them to tell me anything. I know I have cancer," I said matter-of-factly.

"Don't say that!"

"Lori, we need to be real—at least I do. But don't worry; I'm going to be fine."

I probably should have been scared, but mostly I felt a sense of peace and acceptance. I wasn't anxiously waiting for the results. I already knew what the tests would say, and in a weird way, that realization calmed me. Plus, I had faith that God would see me through.

When I got home, I started making calls. My friends and Grandma all reassured me, saying they knew I was fine, that without a diagnosis we didn't know for sure. But while they all tried to sound positive and optimistic, I could hear the anxiety, fear, and concern in their voices. I, on the other hand, remained composed and collected. *Like the calm before the storm,* I thought.

On Friday morning, I chose to get back into the swing of things and finish my Christmas shopping. I wasn't going to wait around for the call. It would come when it came, and I'd deal with it then. So I headed to the mall. I am a firm believer in retail therapy, and there is nothing like shopping for an instant pick-me-up. I hit the Guess store first. I loved Mark for his uniqueness, but his wardrobe definitely needed some help. I figured clothes would make the perfect gift for him. Once I started looking, there was no stopping me. Before I knew it, I was standing in line with a whole new wardrobe in my arms. After I finished paying and was heading out the door, my cell phone rang from deep in my purse. I fumbled with the bags, trying to get to the phone.

"Hello, hello!" I gasped.

"Michelle, this is Dr. A."

My stomach sank. I sat on the edge of a planter in the mall corridor. "Yes?"

"Can you come in to see Dr. G. today?"

"Sure, but tell me why." I knew he didn't want to give me the results over the phone, but I wanted to confirm what I already knew in deep in my bones.

"The biopsy showed cervical cancer. We'll need to do more tests to determine the stage and treatment options."

Even though I had seen this coming for days, I felt like the bottom had dropped out of my world. *I just had a normal Pap test. Can this really be happening?* I was in the middle of the mall with tons of harried holiday shoppers rushing past me, but I felt like everything was happening in slow motion. I was totally emotionless, as if the doctor and I were discussing someone else.

"Where are you?" Dr. A. asked. He sounded worried about me

"The mall."

"Are you alone?"

"Yes, but I'm fine," I lied.

"Okay, will you please come in and see Dr. G. today?"

I agreed. I disconnected with him and called Mark. I needed to tell someone the now-confirmed fact that I had cancer—me, a healthy, active, non-smoking twenty-six-year-old workout nut. Mark didn't answer, but he called right back. I didn't even wait for him to say hello.

"It's cancer! I have cancer!"

There was silence on the line, and then, in a low voice, he asked, "Are you going to die?"

"No!" I snapped. Die? I hadn't even considered the possibility. How could I die? I was only twenty-six. Other than experiencing the usual feminine itch and being a little more tired than usual, I felt fine. I thought my recent exhaustion was a by-product of my hectic schedule. I never considered it might mean something more serious, something like cancer. What was going to happen to me?

The rest of the morning was a blur. Lori was crying when she arrived at my apartment building. I met her in the parking lot and held her until her tears stopped.

"You can't leave me!"

"I'm not going anywhere, Lori. Trust me."

She accompanied me to the appointment with Dr. G. It was set for 4:00—the last appointment of the day. Everyone in the office seemed friendlier than usual. *Did they all know?*

The receptionist led us straight back to Dr. G.'s office. I had known Dr. G. and Dr. T. since I was seventeen, but I'd never seen their personal offices. Apparently this was how it worked when you had cancer. You get special treatment.

"How are you?" Dr. G. asked as we entered the room.

How am I? I hadn't taken time to process everything that had happened over the last few days, so I wasn't sure how to answer that. I sat in a chair facing his desk. "My Pap test was normal just over a month ago. Normal! How can I have cancer?"

Dr. G. told me I had a type of adenocarcinoma: cancer of the cervix that was present in glandular tissue. The Pap test only looked at the surface cells of the cervix. It didn't sample the glandular tissue found in the cervical canal.

"The Pap test is only a screening tool," he said. "It's not 100 percent."

What? Why am I just learning this now? I had put myself through one every year since I was sixteen and thought that meant I was protected. I had never heard this "not 100 percent" business before, and I was pretty sure none of my girlfriends had either. I thought a normal Pap test meant that everything was fine; that I was fine. But it wasn't true and I wasn't fine. I had cancer.

Dr. G. mentioned how relieved he was that he had performed the ECC the day he examined me.

"Isn't that routine procedure?" I asked.

"No." He went on to explain that since the outside edge of my cervix looked normal and healthy when he examined me, protocol didn't require any further testing or procedures. Gut instinct had told him to add the ECC.

Dr. T. stopped in to check on me. She shared Dr. G.'s relief that he had performed the extra procedure. She admitted that she probably wouldn't have done the ECC, since everything else looked good. I didn't say it, but I thought how fortunate I was that she had had an emergency that day. Otherwise they might not have found the cancer until it had spread even farther, and then what?

Before I left, I scheduled an appointment with Dr. A. for December 27. He would determine if any other tests were needed and would describe the cancer and treatment options in more detail.

"What questions do you have?" Dr. G. asked. "How are you doing emotionally? Can we do anything to support you?"

You just told me I have cancer. What do you expect me to say? I'm fine!

I left the office feeling I had no more information than when I'd arrived. I wasn't even clear on why I had gone there. I had no idea what this meant for my future. I didn't even know if I had a future. Taking care of other people was my strength, but in that moment, I didn't have the faintest idea of how to take care of myself.

The Getaway

December 2001

I'd been called a control freak before, and it's true. I hate being told I can't do something. I get that from my paternal grandmother. I grew up hearing her tell stories of courageous women who rebelled against the odds and accomplished great things. My grandmother had earned a bachelor's degree in her forties and then a master's degree. By the time I was born, Grandma was in her fifties and completing her doctorate. She wasn't just a good role model; she was a constant presence in my life. She encouraged my education, taught me that actions speak louder than words, and let me know she loved me by showing up. She was also stubborn and would not take no for an answer. All of this had a profound effect on me.

I had never been good at sitting around and feeling sorry for myself, or waiting for things to happen around me. I was more of a go-getter, a take-the-bull-by-the-horns kind of girl, and my reaction to this cancer diagnosis was no different. I was determined to fight with all the vigor Grandma had taught me.

So I decided to keep my plans for a pre-Christmas celebration in Miami. It was more than just a trip; it was an affirmation that I was taking control of my destiny instead of letting the cancer control me. I was in the stage many people call denial.

No one in my family was happy about my decision, but I wasn't sure what they expected me to do. Cry, panic, sink into a depression? Whatever it was, I wasn't prepared to deliver. I refused to give the cancer any power in my life.

In preparation for my trip, I wrapped Mark's gifts. We hadn't discussed getting each other presents. It was the middle of December, but between the near breakup and the cancer, Christmas hadn't been the main topic of conversation for us lately.

When I arrived at his place, Mark was waiting for me with lit candles and a bottle of wine. I threw my arms around him and squeezed tightly. I couldn't remember ever being happier to see another person. He kissed the top of my head and then grabbed my bags from the hallway. "I thought you were only staying a few days," he said as he dealt with the pile of luggage. "Did you change your mind?"

I smiled and motioned for the large duffle bag. He handed it over as I said, "I have a surprise!" I unzipped the bag and removed all the gifts. Mark's face fell as I stacked the presents on the floor.

"I didn't know we were exchanging gifts," he said, obviously embarrassed. "I didn't buy you anything."

He looked so sad, and I assured him I hadn't bought the gifts because I expected anything in return. Besides, these were more like necessities. He needed a wardrobe makeover, and stat! Mark laughed, his face brightening.

I watched as he opened each package, pulling out jeans, sweaters, long sleeved T-shirts, and even comfy pants for relaxing. I had also bought him MAC face lotion and a Garth Brooks CD. He didn't like country, but two songs on the CD made me think of him and our relationship. Finally we got down to the last two boxes. I handed him the smaller one first. He tore off the wrapping paper, revealing a tan leather journal. On the front was an elaborate image of an ancient tree, roots and all. I thought it was the perfect metaphor for our relationship. We had endured a long-distance relationship, survived a breakup, were starting new lives in Memphis, and now had cancer to deal with. I hoped that like that tree, we were strong enough to weather the storm; that the roots which were taking hold now would see us through whatever the next several months had in store. I urged him to open the cover. On the inside of the cover was a small metal plaque inscribed with the words: *Qu'hier Que Demain*. Underneath those words was the translation: I love you more than yesterday but less than tomorrow.

He looked up at me, his eyes filled with tears. "Thank you, I love it!" he said. I explained that my maternal grandmother had been from France and had worn a gold medallion around her neck inscribed with those words.

"This is the best Christmas ever. Thank you, Michi."

"Oh, I'm not done. I saved the best for last."

He took the box I held out to him and opened it. Inside was a book I had made for him entitled *101 Reasons I Love, Appreciate, and Respect You*. His eyes widened as he lifted the book out and opened it. He attempted to read all 101 reasons, but kept having to wipe his tears away. I just sat watching him, smiling as Garth Brooks played softly in the background. I wanted to bottle this moment and hold onto it forever.

We spent the weekend shopping, eating, taking long walks, hanging out with Janis, and spending hours in bed, holding each other tight. The doctor had ordered me not to have sex, but I didn't want to face the fact that I might be broken. I tried to initiate the deed, even though I was still cramping from my recent procedure. I couldn't stop wondering, *What if sex isn't the same after cancer? What if I can't do it anymore, can't feel anything, can't orgasm?* I was scared, although I didn't want to admit it.

Mark tried to broach the topic of my cancer a few times, but I felt like talking about it would give it the power to affect my plans, my relationship, and maybe my entire life. He even gave me an out on the move to Memphis, telling me he'd understand if I changed my mind.

I made it very clear I was not going to change my mind. I was in control here. I was not putting my life on hold. I had already lined up movers for the twenty-ninth. My things would go into storage and I would stay at my sister's. In January, a friend would fly to Memphis with me to celebrate my birthday and help me find a new apartment. The ball was rolling, and I wasn't about to stop it, not even for cancer.

Mark and I spent my last day in Miami walking around the shops, wasting time before my flight home. Everywhere we went, my attention was drawn to pregnant women and women with children. I felt like someone had reset the lens through which I viewed the world so that it would instantly focus on babies.

In Anthropologie, I spotted a scruffy gray stuffed elephant from across the store. Mark followed as I walked over and picked it up. I rubbed its softness against both our cheeks. Mark was amazed at my attraction to the silly, stringy-looking animal. I named the elephant Elroy and toyed with the idea of buying him, but decided it was impulsive and returned him to the shelf. Besides, I needed to get to the airport.

The next few days were uneventful. I went to work and spent time at the gym, enjoying the break from my classes. School usually consumed all of my free time, but I could see the light at the end of the tunnel. I had three more weeks of this six-week class and a senior paper to write, and then I'd finally be finished. I was excited by the thought of being a college graduate. My degree, long overdue, would be the best present I could give to Grandma. I couldn't wait to see the look on her face when I showed her my diploma.

I was so focused on finishing school and preparing for my move, I hadn't made any holiday plans except to spend a few hours with Lori. On Christmas morning, I lounged around the house and then got ready to head over to Lori's. When I opened the door, I saw on my doorstep a small brown box with no return address. It hadn't been there when I'd arrived home the night before, and there was no mail delivery on Christmas Day. I carried the box inside and quickly cut it open. Inside was Elroy with a bow around his neck.

There was only one person who knew I wanted Elroy. I grabbed the phone and dialed Mark's number. "Thank you so much! I love him!"

"It's not much, but I wanted to send you something."

"He's perfect. But how did you get him here?"

"The mail, how else?"

"But he wasn't here last night and it's Christmas today."

"Guess it was a Christmas miracle."

After I hung up with Mark, I rubbed Elroy against my cheek. I imagined this was what it felt like to touch a newborn baby's soft skin, and then I considered what a weird thought that was. Where had it come from?

I had always been sure I didn't want children. My feelings about motherhood were complicated by my relationship with my own mother. She was not a girly-girl, not into fashion, hair, or makeup. She was the jeans-and-boots type; a tough woman who often carried a gun.

She had left my sisters and me when I was just three years old to drive tractor trailers. When we were still children, she would visit whenever she was in the area, but for years, my father wouldn't let her take us out of the state. I was fifteen the first time I visited my mother's house. Needless to say, we did not have the traditional mother-daughter relationship. Still, I didn't have bad feelings about her leaving. I think she just wasn't ready to be a mother. She had done the most loving thing she could by leaving us with our father and grandmother, whom she knew would stick by us and raise us with love.

But deep down, I worried that I might end up like her. My mother had had two other children before she married my dad, and she had left them too. I couldn't understand how she could abandon all five of us. Was it some emotional defect? What if she had passed it on to me and I didn't know it? I couldn't bear the idea of repeating the cycle, so I decided I just wouldn't have children. Or at least that's what I thought I had decided. But here I was, nuzzling a stuffed elephant and thinking about babies.

Elroy instantly became my new best friend. I slept with him every night. On the outside, I was a strong, confident young woman kicking ass and taking names, but inside I was freaking out. The cancer diagnosis hung over my head, and I was scared to death about my future. Did I even have a future? Moreover, Mark wasn't exactly Mr. Responsibility. A few weeks before he hadn't even been sure he wanted the responsibility of a girlfriend; now he had a girlfriend with cancer. How long would he stick around? In fact, would any man want me, or was I now damaged goods? I tried to push these fears out of my mind and push forward with my "normal" life. I had always been able to control whatever chaos swirled around me through sheer force of will. I was determined that life with this new cancer diagnosis would be no different.

Reality

December 2001 to January 2002

Reality bit me in the butt on December 27, 2001. I was scheduled to see Dr. A., to learn more about my cancer and discuss treatment options. I wanted to go alone, but my family had other ideas. Lori wouldn't take no for an answer. Our dad had died when she was twenty, and she let me know, in no uncertain terms, that there was no way she was going to lose me. And she wanted to be in the loop regarding all things cancer.

My mother was also in town visiting and insisted on coming. I guess I should have been happy she was concerned enough to make the effort, but honestly, the thought of having her there just made me anxious. My sisters had always longed for our mother to take a more active role in our lives, but not me. I was fine with our setup. Needless to say, my mother hadn't attended many of my doctor appointments with me over the years. When she had, I was embarrassed as we debated the facts of my health history in front of the doctor. I always felt she made up details to fill in the blanks of what she had missed by not being in our daily lives.

Even though I dreaded having any of them there, I relented. (Typical middle child, not wanting to hurt anyone's feelings.) I told both Lori and my mother that they could accompany me, on the condition that neither said a word. I didn't want to deal with their drama.

We sat silently in the waiting room. I could feel their anxiety growing with each passing minute, which only made me more uncomfortable.

I wish I were alone.

The nurse eventually led us to the doctor's office. I could practically hear my mom and sister planning what they wanted to say.

I'm going to kill them if they open their mouths.

Dr. A.'s office had no windows. The shelves were stuffed with books. His desk was disorganized, covered with a sliding mountain of patient charts.

Dr. A. started by making small talk, chatting about Christmas, the weather, and the upcoming New Year. Lori mentioned I was moving to Memphis.

"Memphis?" he said. "I just interviewed for a job there. It's beautiful along the river. I can recommend a doctor there. Where are you going to live?"

"I'm not sure," I answered. "I haven't found a place yet, but somewhere downtown. My insurance is here in Maryland, so I don't think I'm ready for a recommendation just yet." While I was excited for the move, I generally hated change. I had been on my father's insurance plan with the same HMO since I was a child, and I wasn't ready to accept the fact that I would need to find new doctors.

After a few minutes, Dr. A. got down to business. He told me again that I had adenocarcinoma: cancer of the glands inside the cervix. He explained it was a rare type of the disease called villoglandular adenocarcinoma, mainly affecting younger women. I flashed back to the conversation we'd had in the pre-op room, when he said the average age of a cervical cancer patient was fifty and I was too young to worry about it. *Bullshit!*

"There isn't much information on this specific form of cervical cancer," he said. "But regardless of your specific type, it is cervical cancer and we must take action." He gave me copies of article summaries about the disease. Then he switched topics and started talking about my options. He recommended taking an aggressive approach: a radical hysterectomy.

"I'm sorry, what?"

"Radical is a type of hysterectomy used only on cancer patients where we remove the uterus, cervix, fallopian tubes, and possibly the ovaries if we deem they've been compromised. Several inches of the vagina and the connective tissue surrounding the cervical area would be removed as well. Finally, pelvic and abdominal lymph node biopsies would be performed to determine if the cancer has spread outside of the reproductive system. If it has, then those nodes would be removed too."

I just stared at him. I wanted to say, "You want to gut me like a pig! What will I have left?" Instead, I said, "I'm twenty-six! Are you crazy? No way!"

He switched tactics. "There are two other ways we could proceed, but I don't recommend either. One option is a scaled-back version of the radical hysterectomy, in which we would only remove the cervix, uterus, and the top portion of the vaginal canal."

Only? Vaginal canal? Umm ... no, thanks. Next.

"The other option is to perform the cone biopsy that we were supposed to do and determine the official stage of the cancer, and then proceed from there."

I was astounded. They didn't know how far the cancer had spread, but they were ready to take everything?

"I'm not having my vagina or uterus cut out," I said. That would change everything: sex, fertility, womanhood—my entire life. I felt like my reproductive organs were a crucial part of what made me a woman. I wasn't about to just hand mine over.

He tried to convince me. "The average woman has about eight inches of vaginal depth, and since the vagina is a muscle, it will stretch. I plan on removing about two inches, leaving plenty of length for sexual intercourse."

He told me that most female sexual pleasure came from the clitoris, and the surgery would not affect that. Without thinking, I shouted, "No, I'm not into just foreplay. I like penetration and deep too. I'm keeping my vagina and cervix!"

Everyone looked at me with shock. *You started it*, I thought. *You're talking about cutting out my girly parts. I'm not going to just keep quiet.*

"The cervix plays no role in sexual pleasure," Dr. A. said. "Once you heal, sex should be normal again."

Normal? I silently raged. *I'm sorry, but do you have a fucking vagina? Better yet, when was the last time someone suggested having your vagina and cervix cut out? Oh, that's right—never! So don't tell me about what you consider "normal."*

I couldn't wrap my mind around what he was saying. I was physically present, but I felt very far away. This doctor was not only strongly suggesting I submit to a radical hysterectomy, he was telling me I could never get pregnant, never have my own biological children. What he was not saying was that my whole life was about to change.

Lori had always been sure she wanted children. In fact, sometimes it seemed like becoming a mother someday was her main goal in life. When we were kids, she played pregnancy while the rest of us played house. Not me. I preferred to focus on school and work, Whenever my ex-husband brought up the subject of children, I changed it. I just couldn't commit to motherhood.

But now that this doctor was telling me he wanted to take my reproductive organs, I was angry. It was easy, even normal, to be ambivalent about motherhood at the age of twenty-six. But how would I feel at thirty or thirty-five? There was no way to tell. So even though I wasn't sure I would ever want children, I was sure I wanted the choice. I was not giving up my fertility!

It dawned on me that there might be more than just medical opinion influencing his recommendation for a radical hysterectomy. This was an HMO, and like all businesses, they were concerned with the bottom line. Their job was to get rid of the cancer in the most inexpensive way possible. If I opted for a more cautious approach now, it might mean more surgeries down the line, which would cost more money. I realized I was the only one in this conversation who was concerned about not just saving my life, but saving my *quality* of life. If I wanted to preserve my fertility, I was going to have to fight for it.

"I'll take my chances with cancer and God," I said. "I will not let you cut out my womanhood."

"Michi, what are you saying?" Lori exclaimed as my mother started crying.

I held firm. "No."

My stubbornness paid off.

"Let's start slowly," Dr. A. said. "I'll schedule the cone biopsy. We'll find out the stage of your cancer and then talk about the next step."

He stressed that this procedure would be diagnostic, but with substantial risk for an incompetent cervix. He was also very clear that this would not be the last procedure he would recommend.

As I sat there trying to process what was happening to me, both my mother and sister pleaded with me to listen to the doctor. I took a deep breath and reluctantly agreed, but only to the cone biopsy.

"Great," Dr. A. said. He consulted his schedule. "Looks like we can get you in on January 2."

Happy New Year to me!

The day after New Year's, Lori drove me to the hospital for the cone biopsy. Afterward, we drove home in silence. Since all of my stuff was in storage, "home" was the three-bedroom townhouse Lori rented with her boyfriend. I called Mark to let him know I was finished and doing okay. He was on his way to Knoxville to prepare for his move to Memphis at the end of the week. We kept the conversation short because I was in a great deal of pain and didn't feel like talking. After we said good-bye, I crawled into bed and fell asleep.

Two days later, Friday, the phone rang early. I looked at the caller ID and knew it was Dr. A. I hesitated before answering. My stomach turned and my palms got sweaty.

"Hello. What are the results?" I asked.

"I'm sorry, Michelle, the margins are positive. It's stage IB1."

"Positive, IB1 … What does that mean?" I asked, trying to stay calm.

"The stage IB1 means the tumor was visible without a microscope. The term positive means the tumor expanded to the edge of the biopsy. There were cancer cells throughout all of the tissue we removed, which means there's likely still cancer in your body. We'll need to perform the radical hysterectomy. It's the only way to make sure we get it all."

"No, I won't do it! I will not give up my fertility," I said as tears streamed down my face.

What he didn't understand was that I wasn't scared of the cancer. I wasn't even scared of dying. I was scared of what life would be like after a hysterectomy. What would it mean to me? To my future? I felt like I had been backed into a corner and had no control.

"Please think about it over the weekend and come see me next week," Dr. A. said gently.

After I hung up, I sat there in shock. I had really thought the cone biopsy would show the cancer was not as bad as the doctors thought, and they would see this whole hysterectomy business as totally unnecessary. Instead, Dr. A. told me the cancer might be worse than they thought. I had no idea what that meant for me, but I did know one thing: I was not having a hysterectomy at twenty-six.

It took a few minutes to digest the news from Dr. A., and then I pulled myself together enough to call Mark. Like my family, Mark wanted me to follow the doctor's orders and have the surgery. I felt weird explaining my perspective to him. I loved him, but our relationship was still new. We had just made the decision to try living in the same city; we were nowhere near discussing children. He had already broken up with me once because he was afraid of responsibility. My health was one thing, but the decision to have children was another issue. I didn't think it was a conversation we could have. I was going to have to make this choice alone.

Research

Cancer has this way of making you feel helpless, but I was determined not to let it win. I was scared, but I was not going to sit around feeling powerless, nor was I going to do as the doctor advised and give up my fertility. It was time to get serious. If I wanted to take back even some control, I needed to learn as much about cervical cancer as possible—and fast.

My last class was wrapping up, and an independent research project was the only thing standing in the way of getting my degree. I phoned my advisor, a former professor of mine, and explained my medical situation. The topic for my paper was supposed to reflect my major, but I couldn't focus on anything other than cancer. I wasn't sure what cervical cancer had to do with organizational management, but I took a chance and proposed doing my research paper on cervical cancer, specifically on the risk factors for developing it and young women's knowledge of the disease. I hypothesized that many young women were misinformed, as I had been, and I wanted to help educate them. I didn't really think my advisor would go for it, and was pleasantly surprised when he agreed.

Feeling more in control already, I phoned a girlfriend and former roommate. Cat worked at the National Institutes of Health, and I asked her about gaining access to their library. She agreed to meet me there in an hour and help me get situated.

I began by researching general information on cervical cancer. I was surprised to learn—based on data from 1998—that an estimated 371,000 new cases of invasive cervical cancer were diagnosed worldwide each year, representing 10 percent of all cancers in women. I was stunned to read that nearly half of those women died. *What did that mean for me? Was I going to die too?*

I kept searching, reading, printing, and highlighting. I needed to become an overnight expert if I was to make the right choices.

Cat and me

I discovered that in the United States, the mortality rates weren't quite as high and the prognosis was more promising. According to data from 1999, 13,700 cervical cancer cases were diagnosed in the US annually, of which nearly 5,000 resulted in death. I pulled out my cell phone and activated the calculator, computing that 36 percent of women who have cervical cancer in the US died from it. *That's one-third!* I was getting scared. (For current statistics see page 169)

I decided I knew enough about mortality rates, so I researched risk factors for developing cervical cancer. Surely doctors knew what made a woman more likely to get this disease.

My maternal grandmother was the only one in our family who had ever had cancer. I knew it had been some sort of female reproductive cancer, but the topic had always been hush-hush, and no one seemed sure if it was uterine or cervical. We only knew she had been diagnosed in her thirties and almost died. When I was younger, I had heard horror stories about her treatment and how it had changed her life forever. Memories of my mom's mother conjured the smell of urine; she always reeked of it. She had undergone both surgery and radiation. Not only did she lose her ability to have any more children, the radiation burned holes in her bladder forcing her to wear an urostomy bag—external bladder—for the rest of her life. I couldn't help fearing I would end up like her, unable to have children and smelling like pee.

As I continued reading, I was shocked to learn cervical cancer was not hereditary. Family history had no bearing. A woman's chance of getting the disease was influenced more by her lifestyle choices than her genes. *Lifestyle choices … Had I done this to myself?* I wondered.

I read through the risk factors: being female (guilty); intercourse before the age of eighteen (guilty); multiple sexual partners (guilty); being with partners who had other partners, especially if those other partners were women who had experienced cervical changes (I didn't know about my partners' partners, but I knew the men I'd been with weren't virgins). I wasn't doing too well on the risk factors, and I wasn't feeling confident about my past choices. There was plenty of information out there about practicing safe sex to avoid contracting a STD or HIV, but I had never heard anyone warn about catching cervical cancer. *Is that what I'm reading: sex did this?*

Confused, I kept reading and learned that exposure to HPV was another risk factor (guilty there too). Some of the literature suggested that a genetic link played a role in determining whether or not the immune system was able to fight off the HPV virus. Some women's immune systems fought the HPV virus, so the women never knew they had it. Others, like me, suffered from a persistent HPV infection, which could lead to cancer. So while cervical cancer itself is not hereditary it appeared the inability to fight HPV just might be.

I recalled that Dr. T. had mentioned that a weakened immune system might be to blame for my repeated yeast infections. Did that also mean my body also couldn't fight off HPV?

Other risks included smoking, having HIV/AIDS, and being of a lower socioeconomic status. I didn't have any of those risk factors. In fact, I was the only member of my family who didn't smoke. What I didn't realize was secondhand smoke put me at risk. The last risk factor on the list was not having a yearly Pap test. *Not me.* I saw the doctor yearly for my Pap test, and even several times in between to treat those dreaded yeast infections. In fact, I had been so diligent about them that I had really thought I was taking care of my reproductive health.

I counted up the risk factors. There were about ten and I had five, but I wasn't sure what that meant.

I wanted to know more about this HPV virus. Of all the factors, that seemed to hold the key. I researched the topic and found that 99.9 percent of all cervical cancer patients had the HPV virus. I was shocked to read studies from college campuses where 50 percent of the females tested positive for

HPV. I recalled Dr. A. saying that anyone who had had sex, even once, was at risk. "If you've had sexual contact with or without a condom since the sexual revolution, you've come into contact with some strain of the virus. It has nothing to do with promiscuity." I hadn't thought much of the comment when he said it, but now it resonated with me.

A persistent HPV infection could cause cell changes in the cervix, which could lead to cervical cancer. I didn't understand everything, but I knew there was that direct connection. I also learned that it could take years for HPV to cause cellular changes or cancer, so it was not possible to know when or by whom I had been infected.

Armed with information about cervical cancer, its risk factors, and the HPV link, I was eager to find everything I could about my options for fighting it. Unfortunately, my initial research was not promising. I found many articles for my stage of cancer, but they all agreed with Dr. A.'s treatment plan—a radical hysterectomy—as the safest course of action and the only way to ensure removal of all the cancer. Even still, it seemed unnecessarily extreme. The cervix was diseased, not my uterus. There was no way I was going to let them throw the baby out with the bathwater. My grandma had used that phrase all the time while I was growing up, and there was a cruel irony to those words now.

The data also mentioned that radiation and chemotherapy were sometimes used for advanced or recurring cases. I didn't think that would apply to me, unless the surgeon, once he operated, discovered that my disease was more advanced.

That is, if I let them operate.

I felt defeated. I had found plenty of information for my twenty-page research paper, but not a solution to my problem. I knew one thing for sure: I was not giving up my choice. I was not having a hysterectomy.

Needing to regroup and ponder my situation, I walked out of the library for a breath of fresh air. Just then my cell phone rang. Lori's number flashed on the screen. I flipped it open.

"Michi, I have it!" she shouted.

"Have what?"

"I've been watching a TV program called Hopkins 24/7. It's about the hospital in Baltimore. There's a surgeon there, Dr. B. He's a gynecologic oncologist and one of the best in the country. He'll know what to do."

I picked her brain for several minutes, attempting to understand why she thought this Dr. B. could help. Lori was a registered emergency medical technician and loved a good medical drama, in real life and on TV. She had watched Dr. B. treat a teenage girl with a cancer of the female organs, and he seemed just as concerned about saving her fertility as saving her life. Plus, Lori rationalized, he must be good if he was on TV. I agreed to give him a try. She set out to find a phone number for his office while I finished my research.

Maybe he did have the answer, I thought. *It sure wouldn't hurt to talk to another doctor.*

Lori's call was the turning point in my day. I returned to the library feeling more hopeful. Oddly, I started uncovering articles about a surgery called a radical abdominal trachelectomy (RAT). The first article was dated October 1997—almost four years earlier. I wondered why no one had mentioned this option.

I read more and learned that the procedure was invented in France, and it preserved fertility in women with early stage cervical cancer. As with a hysterectomy, surgeons removed the cervix, the upper third portion of the vagina, and the parametrium. The key difference was that the RAT left the uterus intact. A clamp was placed at the base of the uterus and the vagina was stitched to the uterus, thus preserving the possibility of conceiving and carrying a child. That sounded like a better option than the hysterectomy. It couldn't guarantee the enjoyment of sex, but at least it provided an option for preserving fertility.

Of the four articles I read, one discussed the option of performing the surgery vaginally rather than cutting open the abdomen. That procedure was called the radical vaginal trachelectomy (RVT) and would leave a much less visible scar. I knew a scar was the last thing I should be worried about, but I couldn't help it. This whole thing was traumatic enough. Did I really need to see a reminder every time I looked in the mirror?

I searched the articles for mentions of where the studies were performed. It seemed the only records of this RAT were in France and Canada. But I figured someone in the US must know how to perform this procedure! I was determined to find him or her.

Monday morning, Lori called Dr. B.'s office at Johns Hopkins and spoke with his assistant. She explained the situation. Dr. B.'s assistant was great and scheduled an appointment for Thursday the tenth, just three days away.

I called Dr. A.'s office for a referral to Johns Hopkins and was told that Hopkins was out of my provider network. The HMO would only grant me a referral if they didn't offer necessary care within their system. Dr. A.'s office felt they could provide the medical care I needed. I disagreed. Determined, I decided to try another angle. Dr. T. had been my gynecologist for ten years— we had history—so I phoned her office and asked for help. She agreed, filled out the form, and faxed it to Hopkins.

Meanwhile, I went to the records department of my HMO and requested

Michelle L. Whitlock

copies of all my medical records dating back to October 2001. I assembled my documents—doctors' notes, pathology reports, and the articles about RVT—into a reference by tabs. I was armed and ready to fight. I wanted the RVT and I felt I shouldn't have to pay for it. This was my health, my future, we were talking about, and I wasn't going to take no for an answer.

70

Options

January 2002

I didn't know how much longer I could keep up the facade of acting like the normal, confident Michi everyone knew. Sitting still was not my strong suit and waiting—waiting to move, to hear my options, to see if I would live or die—was driving me crazy. Inside I knew if I stopped and really absorbed everything that was happening to me, I would fall to pieces. I did my best to hold it all together by staying in constant motion and marching forward, even though I didn't know where the road would lead.

By the time I had my appointment with Dr. B., I was almost sick from anticipation. I felt like he held my future in his hands, and I was eager to hear his opinion. Lori joined me on the forty-five minute drive to Johns Hopkins.

After I had filled out the requisite paperwork, a nurse showed Lori and me to an examination room. The next fifteen minutes felt like an hour. I was ready to jump out of my skin.

Finally a man entered the room. I guessed he was the doctor, but he didn't look like any doctor I had ever met. He appeared to be in his mid-forties. His long brown hair was pulled back in a low ponytail. He wore the traditional white coat, but other than that he looked like a hippie. This was the world-renowned surgeon?

He introduced himself as Dr. B, flipped through my chart, and finally said, "So, what's the nature of your visit?"

What a strange question, I thought. *It wasn't like I was there to order a pizza.*

I explained my situation and my desire to preserve my fertility options. His questions were rushed and short, but thorough. He did not perform a pelvic exam since I was still tender from the cone biopsy a week earlier. Then he told me the magic words I wanted to hear: "I think you may be a candidate for the radical vaginal trachelectomy."

He knows about the RVT and he can to do it! Lori was right. This man must be one of the best.

"But," he continued, "I'll need to see your original pathology slides. I want to make my own determination."

And there was a catch. "The RVT is highly experimental," he went on. "I'm one of the only doctors in the US who performs the procedure, and I've only done twelve. You would be my thirteenth patient. It's not foolproof. The main reason to opt for the RVT over a radical hysterectomy is to preserve your fertility."

He asked me again about my desire to have biological children.

"Yes," I replied. "I'm sure I want children." The truth was I still didn't know, but it was clear Dr. B. needed a definite yes to consider me a candidate. He reemphasized that his pathology team needed to review all the slides and samples from my past procedures. With that he stood, shook my hand, and said he'd call once his office completed its review of my case.

First I contacted Holy Cross Hospital and requested all specimens be sent to Johns Hopkins. Then I notified Dr. A. of my visit to Baltimore and my strong desire to have a RVT instead of the radical hysterectomy. While I hadn't been accepted as a candidate for the procedure yet, I had a good feeling about it. Finally, I started on the red tape I knew I would encounter with my HMO. Dr. B. was not one of their surgeons. The HMO system was tough to navigate, requiring many phone calls and letters, but I needed this treatment and I couldn't afford it on my own.

The HMO declined my request, stating that my plan offered adequate in-house treatment for my condition: the radical hysterectomy. I disagreed. A treatment that would take away my fertility at age twenty-six, before I'd had children, might be "adequate" for them, but it wasn't going to work for me. I was prepared to fight.

Cancer was not my only pressing situation. I was scheduled to move to Memphis in just two weeks and I refused to postpone my plans. Just like I wasn't going to let my HMO take my fertility, I wasn't going to let cancer take this move away from me. If I put my life on hold, then the cancer won, and that was not an option. My family and friends thought I was crazy, but continuing with the move was the only way I knew to keep sane in the midst of all of the chaos.

My friend Andi had agreed to fly with me to Memphis to find an apartment. Andi and I had met at work several years earlier, but I had been her supervisor, which made it hard to socialize. Once she quit, our friendship really blossomed. She later told me, "Quitting was one of the best decisions I ever made. It opened the door to our friendship." We shared a natural connection and could spend hours together just talking and laughing. She knew how to read me and could often tell my thoughts before I spoke them.

Andi-pants and me

Mark borrowed his brother's car to shuttle Andi and me around town. He and his older brother were living in midtown, just outside the downtown area. I wanted to be close enough to see him regularly, but far enough so that we could have our space and separate lives. Downtown was perfect. It was only ten minutes away from where Mark was, but it was a separate neighborhood with its own unique character. The city was renovating the downtown and new communities were springing up along the river. I had always lived in the suburbs, so I loved the idea of being in a city. To me, Memphis's small downtown had the energy of a city, but felt intimate and manageable—the best of both worlds.

Now that I had chosen a part of town, I needed the perfect apartment. I had only this one weekend to make a decision and set everything in motion in order to move the first week in February. My timetable was tight, but I kept reminding myself of one of my favorite sayings: "The next few years are going to come and go. The question remains, what will you have accomplished?" I had heard it on the radio just over a year before, and it had sparked the fire in me to finish my bachelor's degree. Now I used it for encouragement and motivation regarding my move. *There's no time like the present!* I told myself.

The three of us first checked out an area just north of the downtown circuit called Mud Island. Driving north along the main road, we saw apartments on the right and a peaceful green riverbank with a paved trail to the left. Several places were available. They were all nice, but none felt like home to me. Mark turned the car around and headed to his place, where we prepared for an evening out on the town.

The next morning, I said I wanted to check out a few more apartments on the south end of downtown. It was an older neighborhood than we had seen yesterday. Mark and Andi were good sports and accompanied me for round two. We passed run down and abandoned buildings, which made me apprehensive. It seemed like an unlikely spot for a luxury apartment. But just then I looked toward the river and saw a magnificent gated community. I loved the place. The apartment was large enough for all my things, the price was great, and the location at the edge of downtown and along the river was perfect. I had found my new home!

Andi and I returned to D.C. on Monday. Wednesday was my twenty-seventh birthday. Most people dread getting older, but not me. I love my birthdays. I believe each new year brings incredible experiences and greater wisdom. But this year was different. Despite my best efforts not to give cancer control over my life, this was the first birthday I didn't feel like celebrating.

Dr. B.'s assistant called that day to let me know that Dr. B. had reviewed my case with his pathology team at Hopkins, and they agreed I was a good candidate for the RVT. This was the best birthday present ever! Dr. B. wanted to schedule my surgery as soon as possible. I requested a letter stating his medical opinion and recommendation. I was excited, but I knew the biggest battle was still ahead: I needed to get my HMO to approve the procedure.

I called the main office and appealed its decision to deny the procedure. Then I faxed over Dr. B.'s letter along with the articles I had collected, and I pleaded with the head administrator. Mentally, I had strapped on my boxing gloves and was prepared to go round for round with the bureaucracy. Common sense reminded me that all businesses needed to make profits; requesting a HMO to spend money on an alternative approach would be a hard sell. But I didn't care.

Lori and I set out to tag team the administrator. I called several times a day and faxed the letters multiple times. When I wasn't calling, Lori was. Our persistence paid off. A week later we received notice that the HMO had approved the RVT. The sky was clearing. The last few months had felt like slogging through a rainstorm; finally, I could see sun. I called Dr. B.'s office and booked my surgery for February 25.

With all the details set, I left Maryland with Elroy the Elephant to make a new start on the banks of the muddy Mississippi. My mom unpacked and set up the apartment while I got situated at work. Despite our rocky history, there are times when my mom can be totally great. This was one of them. Once I told her what I needed, she jumped in, no questions asked. I don't think I could have done it without her.

I spent the next two weeks adjusting to my new environment. Mark hung out with me several nights after work. As much as I wanted to focus on starting my new life, the surgery date was fast approaching and I needed to make arrangements for it. Mark wanted to fly back to Maryland with me for the surgery, but he was taking classes and working part-time. I knew there was nothing he could do for me in the hospital, so I suggested he stay in Memphis and fly out for the weekend following my surgery. Elroy would be my travel companion. It seemed silly for a grown woman to travel with a stuffed animal, but having cancer at twenty-seven seemed ridiculous too. The truth was, I was terrified.

Surgery

February 2002

My pre-op appointment with Dr. B. was on Thursday, February 21. Once again, Lori accompanied me on the journey. Dr. B. checked my lungs and heart, and palpitated my abdomen. He asked a few questions and reviewed the surgery with me to verify that I fully understood what was going to happen. I ended my day in the lab, where a nurse drew several vials of blood.

The surgery wasn't until Monday, so I had the whole weekend to wait and worry. I was starting to buckle under the weight of my life, and I was having trouble pretending to be fine. Andi offered to take me to the mall for a distraction. As we tried on clothes, my mind wandered. I started to panic, unable to remember if I was having the abdominal or vaginal trachelechtomy. I was sure Dr. B. had gone over this with me, but I couldn't remember the details.

Where would the scar be? I wondered. *Would it be visible when I was wearing a bikini? How badly would it hurt? Would Mark still find me attractive?*

I had cancer, yet here I was in the mall, worried about a scar. I felt so childish. I took Andi's advice to call the doctor instead of agonizing over it all weekend. I found out the surgery would be performed vaginally with a mediolateral episiotomy. The procedure is similar to the episiotomy many women undergo during childbirth, but involves a longer, diagonal incision that goes off toward the left buttock. The information was supposed to calm me, but instead, it gave me more to worry about. *How painful would it be when they cut the sensitive skin of my vagina*, I wondered.

That weekend Andi urged me to talk about my feelings. "It's okay to be scared," she said. "You don't have to have all the answers. Please let me help you." She already knew I was trying to protect Lori and the rest of my family by being a pillar of strength in their presence. I was tired of keeping it all inside and I felt my secrets were safe with Andi. Finally, I opened up and told her everything.

I revealed my ambivalence about motherhood and that I had been holding back with Mark, that I was afraid of scaring him off. We had been dating only a short time, and now I had cancer. How would my illness affect our relationship? Over the years, I had learned that the fastest way to scare off a boyfriend was to talk about living together, marriage, or children. Truth be told, babies and motherhood raced through my head every day now. Mark and I rarely talked about kids. When we did, it was in a general way, not in terms of us having children together. He said he didn't want children, and in one way that was a relief, given my situation. But a part of me feared that someday he'd change his mind about kids ... and then what?

I knew this surgery might not cure the cancer forever, but it would preserve my fertility for now. Dr. B. had informed me that I would need to wait six months before trying to get pregnant post-surgery, but that I should attempt it as soon as possible for the best results. Six months! Who was I fooling? I wasn't ready for children, and neither was Mark. What was I doing?

Andi did her best to support me, but it was a lot for anyone to handle. All she could really do was listen and cry with me.

The next morning, it was still dark when Lori and I arrived at the hospital. We carried a duffle bag, packed mostly with items for Lori, since she planned to stay the night. Of course, I had brought Elroy. I missed Mark, but I knew he needed to be in class, and there was nothing he could really do for me except wait and hope.

Two nurses helped me change into the surgical gown, footies, and a fashionable hairnet. Once I was ready, Lori came in to see me. My anxiety grew and my belly fluttered like a hundred baby birds in mid-flight. I knew the outcome hinged on something bigger than I, bigger than even the surgeon. I had the sudden urge to pray.

"Lori, remember when Daddy said if two people prayed together in Jesus's name, their prayer would be answered?"

"Yes. Do you want to pray together?"

I nodded. I reached for her hands and held on tightly. Lori started the prayer, and I chimed in from time to time. Then we both ended by asking in Jesus's name, just as our father had taught us. One of the nurses then gave me medicine through my IV to help me relax. She told Lori to go get some food and rest. The surgery would take at least six hours.

I awoke groggy and disoriented, and in the worst pain I had ever felt. My body trembled in agony; tears ran across my temples and soaked my hair.

"Please help me! You have to help me," I cried out.

I vaguely recall a woman sitting by the head of my bed. "Just a few more minutes, honey," she said in a soft, compassionate voice. "I'll get you another shot to help with the pain. Deep breaths now."

"I need drugs and I need them now!" I screamed.

I was hysterical. The injections of morphine weren't strong enough to counteract the intense pain. I thought hours passed between doses, although

I later learned it was merely minutes. No matter how many shots she gave me, I needed more.

Friends filtered in and out of my room late into the evening. The drugs made everything fuzzy, so I couldn't concentrate. Later I couldn't remember who had been there and who hadn't. I was irritable and edgy and I didn't sleep at all. I alternated between snacking on crackers for the nausea and obsessing over the next morphine dose. I lay there watching the clock and praying for more painkillers. There was one silver lining: according to the nurse, Dr. B. believed he had gotten all the cancer and considered the radical vaginal trachelectomy a success.

Early the next morning, an intern checked on me and instructed the nurses to prepare me for discharge that afternoon. It was late morning when the nurses finally removed the catheter and asked me to attempt to get out of bed. Initially, I refused. The pain was absolutely unbearable. I didn't know the length of the vaginal incision, but considering the agony I was in, it was no minor cut. After my next dose of medication, I finally agreed to try to make the ten-step trip to the bathroom with assistance. I had to show I could go to the bathroom on my own before they would discharge me.

Lori helped me balance over the toilet. I placed my hands on the seat and Lori held me up by my armpits to prove I could pee. With that milestone under my belt, I decided to try a shower. I turned on the water and stepped into the stall, holding onto the wall for balance. The hot water helped calm me.

A group of interns visited me again in the early afternoon. Not much had changed from my perspective. The pain emanating from my vagina and pelvic region was horrific, and no amount of morphine seemed to reduce it. Later that afternoon I was given discharge papers that instructed "pelvic rest for four to six weeks—specifically no sex, douching, or tampons." *Thanks Captain Obvious!* I didn't need doctor's instructions to figure that out. Using my vagina was the last thought on my mind.

I was shocked they were sending me home, given my pain levels and limited mobility. Then again, the HMO was paying, and it allowed only a twenty-four hour hospital stay for this type of surgery. I reminded myself one more time, this was a business for them. Just before we left, the nurse handed Lori two prescriptions for strong narcotics and an appointment card to see Dr. B. the following week.

I spent the next few days on Lori's couch. I got up only to make the short walk to the bathroom. When Mark came to visit that weekend, I was so glad to see him. It reminded me of my new life in Memphis and all the reasons I had for pushing through the pain and getting better. I forced myself up off the couch and, with Mark's assistance, tackled the stairs so I could take a shower. I normally showered every morning, but it now had been four days and the odor was offending even me. Once I was in the bathroom, I convinced Mark to get me a mirror. I separated my legs, leaned forward, and aligned the small mirror between my pale thighs to view the incision. It was about two and a half inches in length, extending in a diagonal line toward my left butt cheek. The sight turned my stomach and brought tears to my eyes.

The last day Mark was in town, I put on a sweater and a long, stretchy skirt and tied a bandana around my unkempt hair. The doctor had recommended walking, and since the D.C. suburbs weren't so warm in February, Andi drove us to the mall so I could get some exercise. I was embarrassed to be seen in public, but knew I had to push myself to move around. I lasted about fifteen minutes. Mark returned to Memphis, and I spent the next few days on Lori's couch working on my senior research paper, reading articles on cervical cancer, and sifting through the responses I'd received from a survey I'd conducted.

The survey consisted of questions about female reproduction that I had distributed to women I knew. I was amazed by how little most of them knew about HPV, cervical cancer, and even the Pap test. Many women didn't even know what their cervix was, let alone where it was. Most of the women who filled out the survey weren't sure why they had a Pap test every year, but like me, they believed that if it was normal, they were in the clear. Only a few had heard of HPV, and not a single one knew what it was, how it was transmitted, or how it connected to cervical cancer. They certainly didn't know to ask to get tested for it. The only thing the women seemed to know for sure was that they should have an annual gynecological exam, and even then not all of them actually did so.

My follow-up appointment with Dr. B. went well. I was able to sit upright, but it still hurt to urinate. Otherwise, the pain was tolerable, so I requested a milder painkiller. Dr. B. examined the vulva and the incision and reported that all was healing well. He reminded me to get plenty of pelvic rest and to come back in six weeks. He told me I would need follow-up care every three months, including a Pap test.

"A Pap test?" I exclaimed. "That test didn't even find the cancer to begin with. Now you're saying I should trust my life with a Pap test's ability to detect any future cancer?"

"The Pap test is a screening tool," Dr. B. said, trying to reassure me. "It may not be 100 percent effective, but it is effective. There's still a higher than average chance it will detect any future cancer."

I didn't know what to say. This was my life we were talking about. "Higher than average" was not good enough.

Dr. B. quickly changed the subject to the issue of pregnancy. "I suggest you begin trying as soon as the healing period is over. Please keep me informed."

I agreed, even though I knew there was no way I'd be ready to get pregnant in six months.

Healing

March 2002 to May 2003

Healing takes time. How cliché. But some clichés exist for a reason, and I was about to experience the truth of this one. Back in Memphis, I finished my research paper and decided to return to work. Dr. B. had recommended four to six weeks of rest, but I was going stir-crazy. I needed contact with other people, and work was the best distraction I knew.

In early April, I returned to see Dr. B. for my six-week post-op checkup. I brought a notebook of questions: How would they track my condition? How would I know if the cancer came back? What options other than the Pap test were available to detect future abnormalities? What would the procedure mean for any future pregnancy attempts? What was the chance of recurrence? What about sex? Dr. B. answered all my questions, but I didn't learn anything I hadn't already heard or read. He told me the incision had healed, so I could attempt intercourse again, but to try a lubricant if I experienced pain.

His suggestion startled me. Lubricant? I'd never had trouble getting wet in my life. I didn't like the idea that I might need help sexually. It made me feel broken.

I had always considered myself blessed with a healthy sexual appetite, and I wasn't afraid of expressing myself sexually. Mark and I were alike in that way and complemented each other well. I missed our naked time together. Physically, I was ready to get back into our sexual relationship, but emotionally I felt like a different person. I was more hesitant and less comfortable with my body. How would sex feel now, and what if I couldn't achieve the same level of satisfaction? Mark was supportive and didn't push me in any way. He reminded me daily that our relationship was deeper than sex.

One evening, a few days after my appointment with Dr. B., I brought home a bottle of pinot grigio. I was hoping the wine would give me the courage I needed to initiate sex. I had also purchased a small bottle of lubricant, just in case. I still wasn't keen on the idea of needing help in that arena, but I wanted to be prepared. (Little did I know that I'd soon be purchasing the stuff in mass quantities.)

After a glass of wine, I felt more confident and led Mark to my bedroom. Things got hot and heavy, and I was ready to go for it. I took in a deep breath and pulled him into me. I recoiled immediately; the pain was tremendous. We repeated this sequence several times, until Mark finally pulled away.

"Stop, Michi. I don't want to hurt you."

"Fuck!" I yelled in frustration. "It shouldn't be this hard. I want things to be the way they used to be. We never had any issues in the bedroom before."

"Baby, you just had major surgery. Give yourself a break."

He tried to convince me that there was no rush, but I was tired of waiting. I knew it was going to hurt like hell whether we did it tonight or next year. I just wanted to get the first time over with. We lay there in silence until I reluctantly mentioned the lubricant in the drawer next to the bed. He quickly reached for it. Between the lubricant and Mark's gentle persistence, we accomplished what we had set out to do. We tried several positions, but couldn't find one that felt good to me. There were no fireworks for me, just more pain—as if I hadn't had enough yet—but at least we had sex. I couldn't imagine it was much fun on his end either, listening to me scream and knowing it wasn't from ecstasy.

Intercourse wasn't the only thing that caused me pain and discomfort. Even sitting or standing was uncomfortable. I retired my sexy thongs because they rubbed and irritated me. The constant pain dulled over the next few months, but it still hurt during sex, even with lubricant. Positions I had liked before didn't feel good anymore. Mark had to be a lot gentler, and I could no longer handle the marathon sessions we had enjoyed in the past. We were learning the art of the quickie.

In May, I received a call from the editor of the *Johns Hopkins Physician Update,* a trade newsletter sent out to physicians and health care networks. The editor was doing a piece on the RVT as an emerging treatment for cervical cancer. The hospital wanted to feature the procedure and Dr. B. in the fall edition.

"Great," I said. "What can I do to help?"

"We need a face—the face of this disease, of fertility preservation, of this surgery. Will you grant us an interview and photo for the piece?"

"Sure. I'd be happy to." I was so grateful to Dr. B. for all he had done for me. Plus, I hoped that by sharing my story, I could help other women with cervical cancer understand that they had options.

Of the thirteen women who had undergone the same surgery, only one other patient was willing to be interviewed for the article, and she did not want her pictures used. The reporter covering the story told me that most of the other patients were embarrassed about their cervical cancer because of its link to the HPV virus. While I wasn't shouting it from the rooftops,

I wasn't ashamed. I knew the statistics: 80 percent of sexually active adults will contract HPV by the time they are fifty. By those standards, getting HPV seemed as normal as catching a cold. I knew there was a stigma, but that was exactly why I felt compelled to talk about it. I wanted to lift the veil and educate other women—and their doctors—about this new procedure for preserving fertility.

In the meantime, I found out I had received an A on my final project—I was finally going to graduate from college. I decided to skip the graduation ceremony since I had already taken so much time off work while treating my cancer. The ceremony wasn't important to me, only the diploma. I wanted to show it to Grandma. However, the graduation was important to her, so we compromised. I purchased the cap and gown and promised to take pictures in the yard with her. I was so proud and relieved that even in the midst of a major illness, I had pushed through and completed my goal of getting a college degree.

After my appointment in April, the HMO informed me that they refused to pay for any more visits to Dr. B. and instructed me to continue my follow-up care with Dr. A. I was upset but decided not to fight that battle. I had won the most important victory—getting the HMO to pay for the RVT—and that was good enough for me.

The first week of June, I went back to see Dr. B. He surprised me by waiving the fees for my three-month post-op exam after I told him about the HMO's decision. He instructed me going forward to follow up with Dr. A. for my Pap test every three months.

The photo shoot for *Johns Hopkins Physician Update* was also planned for that same week. The photo shoot was nothing glamorous—just a man and his camera at the park next to Lori's house. I wore jeans and my favorite long-sleeved tan shirt. He took several shots and then conducted a short interview. I felt a sense of peace after sharing my story, knowing something good might come from this experience. Slowly, life fell back into place.

In late November 2002, I received terrible news. Dr. B. had died of a massive heart attack. His assistant called me to tell me personally. *Dead!* How could that be? He had been in his late forties! I wasn't prepared to feel as emotional about his passing as I did. I was just his patient. We hadn't even known each other very long. But still the news was devastating. His assistant told me how much Dr. B. had appreciated my willingness to share my story and help spread the word about the RVT. She also told me I was the last RVT he had performed before he died. I was stunned as I realized just how blessed I was to have found him. Why had I gotten the option that so many others wouldn't?

Grandma and I holding our own graduation ceremony

I began to question if I was meant to have children. For once I pondered more than just the abstract idea of choice and realized I wanted to be a mother. Deep in my heart, I believed it was no coincidence that I had met Dr. B. and that I had been his last RVT. He had given me a gift, and I intended to use it.

Mark had claimed from the beginning that he didn't want children, and I had accepted that when we first started dating. But things had changed, and I struggled to reconcile that agreement with all the new developments in my life. After just ten short months in Memphis, Mark and I had bought a house and moved in together. We were starting to build a nest and all of a sudden, I felt the urge to fill it. I knew Mark still wasn't interested in marriage or children, so I kept my internal struggle from him. Instead I confided in Andi and Janis, sharing with them how Dr. B.'s death had altered my perspective about motherhood and my concerns about Mark's take on the matter.

I had had three checkups with Dr. A., and all three Pap tests were normal. By February 2003, with the cancer in remission for one year, I changed my insurance and found a doctor in Memphis. Dr. C. would track my progress going forward. Like Dr. A., she was skeptical about the choice I had made to have the RTV. She felt it was too new, too risky, and she feared I might suffer a recurrence. She encouraged me to have children right away.

"You need to get pregnant and then let me have your uterus!" she would say, half joking, every time I saw her.

But I was scared to death to bring it up with Mark. I wanted to be a mom someday, but I wasn't sure if someday meant now. Life was pushing me in a direction I wasn't ready for, but the clock was ticking and I needed to make a decision. I tried not to think about it, telling myself that when the time was right, it would happen. I focused on enjoying my time with Mark, nurturing the new puppies we had just adopted, and working. Little did I know the clock was ticking faster than I could have imagined.

PART III
Everything After

April 2004 to spring 2007

The Morning After —————————————————

April 2004

A year came and went fast, and before I knew it, my two-year checkup was upon me. What I didn't know when I left for that appointment was that I had entered the most pivotal, emotionally charged week of my life. So much so, in fact, that I look back on my life as being split between everything that came before that week and everything that came after. In that brief period of time, I experienced the most happiness I had known with my engagement—and the deepest sadness with the return of my cancer. It set in motion the events that taught me about real love, vulnerability, self-acceptance, and how to let others in and to lean on them.

Let me refresh your memory. Just days after Mark proposed to me, I got the call that shattered my world.

"Michelle, this is Dr. C. Please give me a call back at the office as soon as you get this message."

With those two simple sentences, my worst fears came true. While I was shocked and stunned, Mark was optimistic that I was wrong. He was sure a simple conversation with Dr. C. in the morning would alleviate my fear. But I knew the meaning of her message, and I knew it would send the fairy-tale wedding Mark and I were planning on a major detour.

That night I barely slept, tossing and turning in anticipation of the devastating news. Mark and I were settled and happy. I still hadn't convinced him that we should have a baby someday, but I could see our future together and it looked amazing. How could this be happening?

At 7:30 the next morning, I paced the house while Mark showered. I was nauseous and my hands shook uncontrollably. I wasn't sure what time Dr. C. arrived at work, but I guessed 8:00 would be a good time to call. Mark was scheduled to work at 9:30, and he was preparing the same way he would any other day. Not me. For once, work was the *last* thing on my mind. I paced back and forth, watching the minutes tick by until the clock indicated 8:00 exactly. I picked up the phone, dialed, and listened to the ring.

"Dr. C. speaking."

"Hello, this is Michelle Coots. You left me a message."

There was a long, silent pause, then, "Yes, I'm so sorry. I have your preliminary pathology readings here. The Pap test looks normal. However, the ECC shows at least carcinoma in situ, which means a spot of cancer not yet invasive, although I suspect it probably is invasive. You'll need to go ahead and have a hyster—"

"*Stop!*" I cut her off. "Don't say it. I don't want to hear that word. Not now!"

"Michelle, it's the only option left."

"I will not have this discussion now. I just can't." My voice cracked as tears rolled down my cheeks.

Mark was staring at me, listening to every word I said. He knew instantly by my reaction that I had been right—my cancer was back. Dr. C. insisted I come to her office immediately to have a CAT scan and to speak to her in person. I reluctantly agreed to undergo the scan at 10:30 and meet with her afterward. I ended the call and dropped to the floor. I needed a few minutes to digest my new reality.

Mark called work and arranged to take the day off. I sat on the floor and cried. *How the hell could this be happening? Dr. B. had told me he got all the cancer. He had been so confident that I was cancer free.* I conveniently forgot the part where he also told me the surgery was still considered experimental and there were no guarantees.

I recalled all the normal Pap tests I'd had in the two years since my surgery. How long had the cancer been there? I had followed my checkup schedule faithfully, seeing the doctor every three months like clockwork. Was I going to die?

I was hysterical at this point. Mark sat behind me, wrapping his legs and arms around me in an attempt to comfort me. Even with him there, I felt so alone. There was nothing he could say, and he knew it. Instead of trying to cheer me, he joined in my sorrow. In an instant, he and I had been transported from engagement bliss to the depths of hell.

We arrived at the clinic and went straight to the radiology area to wait for the CAT scan. A nurse ran an IV line into my arm and gave me a pasty shake to drink. It was some sort of contrast dye to help the CAT scan identify trouble areas. As I entered the testing room, the nurse asked me to remove any jewelry I was wearing as I entered the testing room. Like a microwave, the machine didn't care for metal.

The only offending thing on my body was the underwire in my bra. I took it off. Then I lay on the cold table and pulled my pants down below my hips. The table slid back and forth inside the circular machine for several minutes while I tried to lie completely still. The technician injected contrast dye into my IV line, and again the table slid in and out of the machine. Minutes later I was told to dress. As I walked out of the room I felt dizzy and queasy. I passed a mirror and noticed three small bumps under my right eye. While I stared at myself, the individual bumps swelled into one huge welt. Panic rose from my stomach to my throat.

"Problem. I have a problem!"

I had no idea what was happening to me, but I knew I was in trouble. It was as if all the fear I had tried to push down since Dr. C. first left me that damn message was manifesting in my face. The technician grabbed a nurse and rushed me to a bed. The nurse injected Benadryl into my IV line and told me I was allergic to the contrast dye. The Benadryl stopped my allergic reaction but made me very sleepy. I struggled to keep my eyes open, feeling woozy and out of control. That was a perfect metaphor for what was about to happen to my life.

An hour later, Mark and I sat in Dr. C.'s office, bracing ourselves for the worst.

"The ECC biopsy I performed last week shows at best carcinoma in situ," she said. "The CAT scan doesn't show a tumor per se, but we can see what appear to be atypical fibroids—benign tumors in the uterus. I strongly feel that this is in fact a tumor. We probably caught it just in time."

Dr. C. kept talking, but the words went in one ear and out the other. I didn't want to hear what she was saying. I had done my research the first time around; I knew she would recommend a radical hysterectomy with lymph node dissection. She told me failure to act would cause the cancer to spread and eventually kill me. It was not a question of if, but when.

Her words echoed in my mind—the cancer would kill me. Talk about brutal honesty. I could become infertile at twenty-nine or die. Those were my choices.

I was overloaded and completely unable to cope. Dr. C. could tell I was struggling. She handed us a few pamphlets to take home and offered May 4 or 11 as possible surgery dates.

"No, I'm getting married, not having surgery," I said. "I've heard this all before. My wedding is set for June 18. We are leaving on the fifteenth. I can't have surgery."

Dr. C. looked stunned. "We are talking about your life! Please go home and think this through. I'll see you early next week."

Mark and I didn't speak the whole way home. When we reached the house, I climbed into bed and pulled the covers up over my head.

The next day, I kicked into full emotional survival mode. Pushing down all the fear and anxiety, I put on my best game face. I called friends and family members and told them the bad news as if it were happening to someone else. Andi and Caryn immediately announced they would come take care of me.

Like Andi, Caryn had become family. In fact, we often fought like sisters, but in the end, we always made up and supported each other. I loved her crazy, sometimes obnoxious, in-your-face personality.

I tried to rationalize putting off the surgery or ignoring the cancer altogether. I told myself the Pap was normal. The CAT scan didn't show anything other than fibroids. *Fibroids are not the same as cancer.*

I wanted to prove Dr. C.'s opinion about the CAT scan wrong. I read some literature that suggested an MRI might be better for identifying cervical cancer, so I called Dr. C.'s office to schedule an MRI.

"Wednesday, how's that?" the nurse asked.

"Great."

"Okay, Wednesday it is for the MRI, and Friday for your follow-up with Dr. C."

I hung up and wondered why the doctors hadn't performed any of these scans on me the first time they diagnosed my cancer. No one had even mentioned them. *Thank God I'm doing my own research.* I thought. It was another good reminder of how important it is for patients to play an active role in their own health care.

On Friday, Mark accompanied me to my doctor appointment. Dr. C. informed us that the MRI didn't show any clear evidence of a cancerous tumor. The radiologist labeled some abnormal tissue as possible fibroids. In 1999, my OB/GYN had told me I had fibroids, so it wasn't a surprise that the scan might have found some. Dr. C., however, still believed these "fibroids" appeared atypical and were most likely a cancerous tumor. She again urged me to schedule surgery for May.

I pushed back, choosing to focus on the scan's inconclusive results rather than on the damning biopsy report.

Dr. C. tried a different tack "You may be able to keep your ovaries if they appear unaffected during surgery," she said. "Even with just one ovary, you could potentially harvest eggs in the future." She offered me the name of another cervical cancer patient, Kristi, who had already harvested her eggs, fertilized them with her husband's sperm, and frozen the embryos. Reluctantly, I took Kristi's number.

Dr. C. was firm with me: the surgery was my best chance of survival. I wasn't convinced, but I finally agreed to consider having the surgery—after my wedding. She pulled out a calendar and counted the weeks: eight. I could see the disappointment on her face. I knew she thought I was making a mistake, but I wouldn't budge. I wanted to enjoy my time, get married, have a honeymoon, and live my life. She couldn't guarantee having a radical hysterectomy would save me, but I understood it was my best shot at survival. Hesitantly, I authorized her to schedule the surgery for June 28, although I wasn't sure I'd go through with it.

Coping

May 2004

I tried to go on with living, making wedding plans and being happy, but the cancer followed me like a dark cloud. I threw myself into work, filling my mind with other people's problems. Staying busy helped for a few hours here and there, but the reality caught up with me whenever I got in the car. As part of my work, I would spend hours driving between retail locations, through areas without decent radio stations, and the dread pounced as soon as I was alone with my thoughts.

May was a terrible month for my driving record. I was pulled over three times by the police and issued speeding tickets. I wasn't watching where I was going and I didn't even know who was driving most of the time. I often found myself on autopilot, not remembering how I got from one place to another. On the outside, I tried to keep up the usual strong facade, but inside I was unraveling.

Caryn was one of the few people who picked up on my internal struggle. She had called every day since she had first heard about my cancer. I looked forward to our conversations and to the sense of normalcy they brought to my upside-down world. She was a great sounding board; she challenged me and asked questions to be sure I was considering all the options. She openly shared her opinions but didn't shove them down my throat. Thank God. She was known for being over the top and pushy. On days I didn't want to talk, she did the talking, updating me on the latest drama in everyone else's lives. It was just what I needed. Other friends had stopped sharing, apparently deciding their problems were trivial compared to mine. I knew they were trying to be sensitive, but it actually had the opposite effect. It made me feel like an outsider, reminding me that I was not like normal people with normal problems. I was sick, broken.

Initially, I didn't tell my coworkers about the cancer. I didn't want them to treat me differently and I didn't want it to affect my ability to get promoted. I had recently interviewed for an internal position as a district manager. I was so close to getting it and I had worked too hard to let cancer stop me now.

Caryn and I

The district manager who was supposed to be training me was in the hospital, so I couldn't ask him for advice. He had been diagnosed with stage IV brain cancer the same week I learned my own cancer was back. The managers and employees we supervised were upset about his sudden illness, but I had known something was up with him for months. He had lost an incredible amount of weight, he suffered headaches, and he complained about a debilitating pain in his left arm. Still, he refused to see a doctor, chalking it all up to high blood pressure. My friends often teased me that I ran to the doctor for every ache and pain, but now I couldn't help but wonder if that persistence had saved my life.

My employees needed a leader, and I wanted to be strong for them. I hesitated to discuss my diagnosis, knowing it would be a double whammy, but my secret would eventually come out. I decided to come clean.

I called my boss, the director of retail operations, and told him my news. I also conveyed my fear that having cancer might jeopardize my career. He assured me it wouldn't affect a promotion or my standing within the organization. Greatly relieved, I felt as if a fifty-pound weight had been lifted off my shoulders.

Meanwhile, Mark and I discussed my fertility options. He told me kids didn't matter—all that mattered was spending forever with me. He wanted me to have the surgery and save myself, and my stubbornness about the treatment was tearing him apart. He was consumed with fear, and he was in a terrible position. The cancer had profoundly affected his life, too, but he didn't get to choose how to fix it. All he could do was wait and hope I did the right thing—whatever that was.

I hated watching him worry about me. I knew deep down I needed to have the surgery, but I resisted. When I first began my battle with cancer, I hadn't known if I wanted children. I had fought for the option to make that decision later in life. Now I felt that having children was more than a choice; it was my destiny. Of all the women with this disease, I was one of the few lucky enough to find a surgeon who had offered a procedure to save my fertility, and to give me hope. If I wasn't supposed to be a mother, why had I found Dr. B.? Why had I had the radical trachelectomy instead of the hysterectomy? Why had I met Dr. B. just a few months before he died? I was sure it all meant something. I just didn't know what.

I decided I needed a second opinion. Technically, this would be a fourth opinion, if I counted the number of oncologists I'd seen since my original diagnosis. I had heard Dr. D. was the best gynecologic oncologist in the area. I had wanted to see him when I first moved to Memphis, but he didn't accept my insurance. But insurance or no insurance, I needed his opinion. I set an appointment for the morning of May 13. Again, Mark shifted his schedule to come with me. Dr. D.'s office was much smaller and more intimate than the other oncology centers I'd visited, and it was packed with patients. The lady at the desk was particularly nice. I filled out my new paperwork and gave her copies of my medical records. I discovered an added bonus: Dr. D. now accepted my insurance.

We were quickly called back to an examining room. The nurse took my vitals but left without playing the usual twenty questions with me. A woman in a doctor's white coat came in. She introduced herself as a medical student and began asking questions. I got it now. She was the one who'd play twenty questions and gather information for the doctor.

She scribbled notes on my chart and then left Mark and me alone in the room. I was getting anxious. When we heard voices outside the room, I got up and walked over to the door. My gut told me that whoever was out there, they were having a conversation about me. I didn't like the idea of people standing on the other side of the door talking about me, debating my future. I wanted to yell, "If you have something to say, come and say it to my face!"

The chitchat continued, although it was hard to decipher words through the door. I cupped my hands over my ear and leaned in closer. Mark looked at me as if I were losing my mind. Then I heard the door handle rattle and jumped back, attempting to compose myself as the doctor and student walked in.

"We were just talking about you," Dr. D. said with a smile.

"I heard." *I'm so embarrassed! He knows I was eavesdropping!*

He motioned toward the chairs. "I'm Dr. D. How can I help you today?"

I sat down and explained my case again. He personally knew all three of my oncologists, even the two in Maryland. We talked about Dr. B.'s passing and the great loss it was to the gynecology-oncology community. I liked Dr. D. immediately. He had an ease about him unlike any other doctor I had met. He seemed like a real person, with real emotions and real empathy. Eventually, it was time for him to lay the cards on the table. While I braced myself emotionally for the harsh reality that was coming, I was secretly holding out for a miracle.

He sat directly in front of me on a round stool with wheels. He leaned in, intruding on my personal space, but it didn't bother me. His compassion enveloped me.

"You are going to be a wonderful mother someday," he said. "But this is not the way. We have to save your life and then think about fertility. Will you let me help you?"

I nodded yes as the tears spilled down my cheeks. His advice was the same as all the other doctors had offered, but his approach was different. He showed his emotions and spoke to my heart, not just to my mind. I felt like he saw me, the person full of fear, not just a cancer patient. He handed me a tissue and then pulled out a piece of paper to draw the female reproductive system.

"We can do this together," he said. "You'll need a radical hysterectomy, including removal of both your ovaries and a partial vaginalectomy to be sure we get it all. I will do a lymph node dissection and possibly remove both the abdominal and pelvic nodes. At this point, I do not believe you will need chemotherapy or radiation."

"My ovaries too? I want to keep them. The other doctor said I could keep them."

Dr. D. explained that adenocarcinoma of the cervix was sometimes affected by estrogen, which is produced in the ovaries. Since I was suffering from recurring cancer, our best option was to remove my ovaries. I didn't want to surrender them. I pushed back, pleading with him to reconsider. He agreed to leave the ovary option open. He suggested doing a frozen biopsy during surgery, which the pathologist would review in the operating room. He agreed to call Mark during the surgery after the biopsy was performed, and Mark could decide whether to keep my ovaries. Dr. D.'s willingness to compromise helped me swallow that nasty pill.

"How will you cut me?" I asked.

"Vertically from the pelvis upward, around the belly button to the sternum."

"No way! It's bad enough to go through all this, but I don't want an ugly reminder staring back at me in the mirror. You'll have to cut horizontally, hip bone to hip bone and hand-sew every layer, no staples."

He looked shocked at my demands. "You can have a plastic surgeon in the room if you want."

"No plastic surgeon. Give me your word and I'll let you do it. I'll trust you."

He nodded. "We have a deal."

"And I can't do it until I come back from my wedding. I need to get married first. I want to start my new life and enjoy my wedding day."

We pulled out a calendar and selected the Monday after my honeymoon for surgery. Dr. D. was reluctant to put off my surgery, but agreed to wait until the end of June. I looked at the date, June 28, and realized that ten short days after the wedding, I would be on the operating table. I started crying and looked at Mark. His eyes were overflowing with tears too.

"What about freezing eggs?" I asked.

Dr. D. grabbed his phone and looked up the number for Dr. K., who owned a fertility clinic in town. I took the phone number but declined his offer to set up an appointment. I was too drained to decide anything else now. Besides, I had no clue how I'd pay for that too. Dr. D. said he would call ahead and tell Dr. K. about me, in case I changed my mind about seeing him. As Mark and I headed out the door, I looked up at the clock. We had been there for an hour and a half. Doubtless, Dr. D. was behind on his schedule now, and I was grateful for the time and attention he had given me. He had made me feel like I was his only patient, his only concern. As I stood in line to set my next appointment, Dr. D. opened the door to the lobby.

"I'm running behind today, ladies. I want to give each of you the time you need, so please be patient with me."

Mark and I looked at each other, stunned. I was all too familiar with doctors' offices, and I had never witnessed anything like Dr. D. I was sure he was the right person for the job.

Maybe Babies

May to June 2004

The phone number for the fertility specialist, Dr. K., lay on my nightstand all weekend. I'd pick it up every morning and again every evening. I'd stare at the number, unsure of what to do with it. I assumed harvesting eggs was pricy and I was afraid to approach Mark with the topic. He had always been upfront about not wanting children, and nothing had happened to make me think he had changed his mind. Monday morning I sat in bed holding the number, trying to muster the courage to broach the subject with Mark. I was terrified that not only would he say no, he would be unwilling to even discuss the option.

"What are you doing, sleepyhead?" he shouted from the kitchen. "Breakfast is coming." He entered the room with a bowl of Fruit Loops and placed it by my side of the bed.

I grabbed his hand, pulling him down onto the bed. I handed him the number. "I want to call and see what it costs."

"Okay. Make an appointment."

I was shocked and relieved. I grabbed the phone and dialed the number. The receptionist told me I could be seen in two weeks.

"*Two weeks!* I have cancer!" I blurted out. She put me on hold and then returned a moment later to offer me a slot for Thursday morning, May 20.

At least having cancer was good for something, I thought.

I arrived at the office feeling uncomfortable and insecure. I didn't even know what questions to ask. The waiting room was quiet, and the receptionist asked me to fill out more paperwork. Why didn't all doctors use the same forms? Then the patient could fill out the paperwork just once, keep a copy, and present it at each different office.

Eventually they called my name, and after taking the usual vitals, a nurse led me to an office. Dr. K. entered shortly thereafter. I introduced myself as a patient of Dr. D. and told him about my latest cancer diagnosis. He reminisced about first meeting Dr. D. during his residency in Houston. Then he told me how he had almost lost a very sick patient, but Dr. D. stepped in and helped save her. The admiration and respect they shared was evident. After he finished his story, I gave him the details of my situation.

He explained the process for harvesting eggs. It was quite involved, including many tests and examinations, plus a regimen of birth control pills to regulate the patient's cycle. "When are you having surgery?" he asked.

"June 28."

He gaped at me. "There's no time to waste. We better get started! We'll have to make a few assumptions due to the tight time frame. We'll assume you're perfectly fertile, except for the cancer. Before you leave, we'll need to do some blood work, an ultrasound, and a screening for sexually transmitted disease."

He handed me a sheet with a breakdown of the cost. He crossed off some of the tests listed—he'd assume all those were fine. I looked at the prices on the sheet and quickly did the math: it was going to cost somewhere in the neighborhood of $15,000. *There's no way I can afford this.*

I didn't have that kind of cash and definitely didn't have time to save it in the next six weeks. My head was spinning. Everything was coming at me so fast. *Do I start the process today? Do I go home and talk to Mark?* I didn't know what to do.

Dr. K. spoke. "I'll donate some of the necessary medicine, given the circumstances of your situation. Besides, I still owe Dr. D. for saving my patient all those years ago."

I took his generosity as a sign. With that, my rational mind checked out for the day and I acted on pure instinct, accepting the donation and having the preparatory tests done. I left the office with a bag full of donated fertility drugs in need of immediate refrigeration.

Questions whirled through my head. Where would I get the money to pay for this? The donation helped, but I knew I still needed thousands of dollars to make this a reality. What was I going to tell Mark? Would he even be willing to give me his sperm when he didn't want children? There was a big difference between investigating the options and saying, "Okay, honey, I need your sperm *now* to make a baby."

When I arrived home from work, Mark was in the kitchen preparing dinner. "Honey, what's the big brown bag in the fridge?"

"Oh, yeah, the bag." I hesitated and then started talking a mile a minute, trying to explain. "They were a gift from Dr. K. He gave me these drugs to help with the cost, but we have to get started right away."

"What? Slow down, baby."

"I need you to go to the doctor tomorrow. All you need to do is give them a sample of your sperm for analysis, okay?"

I opened my eyes wide, silently pleading with him. He pulled me close, kissed my forehead, and asked me to tell him more. I explained everything I had learned about harvesting eggs, presenting it as a safety net: in the future, he might change his mind about having children, and this would give us the option.

"It doesn't mean we have to have children," I said. "We can decide that later." I said. My mind was working overtime, thinking of how to convince him to go along with this crazy, spur-of-the-moment roller coaster I'd put us on. I wanted him to ride the ride and ask questions later—much later. I didn't have answers and I didn't have time to find them. For once in my life, I was just going with it, whatever "it" was.

Then I pulled out the sheet with the financial obligations. Mark's jaw dropped. "You're talking about over ten thousand dollars! Does insurance cover any of this?"

"Not really. I think the maximum lifetime benefit for infertility is only three thousand." I couldn't bring myself to make eye contact with him.

He tried to speak to me rationally, explaining that we already faced a mountain of medical bills with the cancer. I heard what he was saying, but I couldn't put a price on this. Not this. I pleaded with him not to worry about the money. I would figure it out. I just couldn't make the decision based on money. This was too important, my only chance to have biological children.

Before the weekend was over, we agreed that Mark would go to the doctor and ask his own questions. He would start the testing process, referred to as the husband investigation, while I figured out the financial side. I convinced him that we weren't committed yet, but at least all the preliminary stuff would be out of the way.

Mark called me as soon as he finished his appointment. He had had to provide sperm. Hearing the weirdness in his voice, I urged him to give me all the juicy details, trying to lighten the mood by asking questions about the girls in the magazine he had used. We shared a few laughs before returning to our busy days.

The next day I went back to the fertility center. I needed to learn how to inject myself with the donated drugs. The nurse flipped open my chart and stopped. "Dr. K. needs to speak with you before we go any further."

Dr. K came in a few minutes later and dropped a bomb in my lap. He had talked to Dr. D. and there was a problem. Dr. D. had explained that hormonal increases could affect the cancer. Since the drugs used to induce ovulation would definitely increase my estrogen levels, the cancer could become much more invasive between now and the surgery date. Dr. K. made it clear that this created an ethical issue for him because he couldn't be certain how my body would respond to the fertility treatment. He didn't want to cause me any harm or risk my life. I calmly listened and digested the information. When he finished speaking, I surprised even myself by telling him that it was fine to proceed. I assured him that he had done the right thing medically by warning me about the risk, but that ultimately it was my life and I wanted to move forward. After verifying that I understood what was at stake, he reluctantly agreed.

The nurse pulled out a vial of saline and a syringe. First she showed me how to fill the syringe with fluid from the vial. That was the easy part. Then she wiped a small area on my stomach with alcohol. She pinched the area together and injected me with the saline. I cringed as the needle pierced my skin.

"Now it's your turn. I need to see you give yourself one injection before we can begin."

I removed the protective cover from the needle, turned the vial upside down, and inserted the needle. The nurse wiped the alcohol pad across my stomach again. I took a deep breath, aimed the needle, and jammed it into my skin.

"Congratulations, Michelle, you are certified on injections! Stop taking the birth control pills today, and Friday you will begin giving yourself the shots at home." With that, she escorted me to the checkout desk and waved good-bye.

Now that that was done, I needed to find a wedding dress. I left the fertility clinic and went directly to David's Bridal. I wasn't sure what I was looking for, but I figured I'd know when I saw it. Unfortunately, there were about a million dresses to sort through. I needed help.

I left in a panic and headed across the street to the mall. While I was confused about my own wardrobe, I knew the perfect look for Mark. I searched high and low for white linen pants and a casual linen shirt. The ceremony was going to be on the beach, and neither of us planned to wear shoes.

I spotted the perfect outfit for him and purchased it, and then I called him and asked him to meet me at the bridal store. I knew the old saying about it being bad luck for the groom to see the bride's dress before the big day, but from where I was sitting, my luck could only get better. Besides, every girl needs her best friend to help her pick a dress, and Mark was my best friend. We sifted through the prom dresses and bridesmaid dresses, looking for one simple enough for a beach wedding. When the sales clerk lifted one up for us to see, I exclaimed that that was the one.

The dress was a slim silhouette that flared slightly just below the hips. The spaghetti straps lay gently on my shoulders, and the embroidered flowers accentuated my bust line. I walked out of the dressing room and twirled in front of Mark.

"That's it, baby!"

I walked through the door just after 6:00 p.m. with my arms full of packages from my day of shopping. My cell phone rang deep in my purse. I dumped the shopping bags on the kitchen counter and scrambled through my bag for the phone. "Hello, hello!"

"Michelle, it's Dr. D."

"Is everything all right?" Just hearing his voice raised my anxiety level.

"I'm concerned about your choice to proceed with the egg retrieval before your surgery."

"Well, if you take my ovaries during surgery, then I won't have a chance. I need to do this now."

He reviewed the risk with me again, emphasizing that the drugs used to induce ovulation could very well cause the cancer to spread and greatly worsen my condition. I asked him for specific statistics, but he couldn't provide them. He wouldn't know the exact extent of my condition until after the surgery, so he could not tell me how my body or my cancer would respond to the fertility stimulation. I told him I understood and accepted the risk. Then he reviewed with me the treatment plan for after the wedding. I was prepared to hear him say he would be performing a radical hysterectomy. I was not prepared to hear him mention radiation and chemotherapy.

"What radiation and chemotherapy?" I snapped. "I thought you said my cancer was probably still in the early stages and surgery would take care of my condition!"

He tried again to reason with me, reiterating that we didn't know the extent of the disease and that the medications used to induce ovulation might have an adverse affect on the cancer. Plus, there was another risk. The needle used to aspirate the eggs could spread the cancer.

What? This I didn't know.

He explained that in order to retrieve the eggs, a large needle would be inserted vaginally and then would pierce the vaginal wall and the ovary. If the needle came into contact with a location containing cancer, it could spread cancer cells. I sat down and took a deep breath. Hearing the words radiation and chemotherapy made the whole situation feel a thousand times worse. I thanked him for his concern and got off the phone.

Radiation, chemotherapy. I hadn't considered either of those as treatment options. My heart raced as I questioned my decision. Without any further thought I stood up, walked to the mirror, and looked myself in the eye. I would stick with the plan. I would not give in to fear. I would start the process of harvesting my eggs. Mark was on board whether he wanted to be or not, and I was getting married. I pushed the other thoughts from my mind and marched forward.

I phoned Grandma. She had always been in my corner, cheering me on and picking me up when I fell. After all, she signed my birthday cards, Grandmother by birth, mother by choice. I hated to ask, but I knew I had no other option for getting the money I needed to make this all a reality. My grandmother agreed to send me $3,500 to assist with the fertility fees. The donated medicine was worth a couple thousand, and insurance might help with up to $3,000. That left more than $7,500 unpaid. I decided there was no turning back now. I pulled out the credit cards, checked the balances and APRs on each one, and made my selection. It wasn't ideal, but I didn't have any other option.

On Friday the shots started. That night I laid the supplies across the kitchen table. Mark was in the bedroom getting ready for bed. I prepared the syringe just as the nurse had shown me. Then I pulled up my shirt and wiped a spot with alcohol. I made a fist around the syringe and aimed for my gut, but the needle barely penetrated the skin. My stomach felt rock hard. I attempted to jam the needle in again, but it didn't work. I yelled for Mark. He didn't come immediately, so I yelled again. He flew around the corner, asking, "What is going on in here?"

"I can't get the needle in," I cried. My emotions were running high. "I need you to stick it in."

"Oh, I'll stick it in all right," he teased.

"I'm serious. Will you give me the shot? My stomach muscles are strong, so push hard."

He stabbed me with the needle like I was a piece of meat.

"Ouch!"

"You said hard."

"Not that hard."

At least the needle was finally in. I pushed the plunger, forcing the medicine under my skin. It occurred to me we had just finished finalizing our vows. But I would bet this wasn't what Mark had pictured when he agreed to "for better or for worse."

On Monday, the nurse called with the results of Mark's sperm analysis. "The volume, or quantity, of sperm collected was great. However, there is a slight problem. The progressive mobility and morphology is poor." I had no idea what she was saying. "This condition greatly decreases the likelihood of fertilization without assistance."

"What does that mean?"

"The shape of the sperm and the speed at which they swim is poor. You'll need intracytoplasmic sperm injection to ensure the best possible odds of fertilizing the eggs."

I wasn't exactly sure what she was telling me, but I guessed it meant more money. "What's the cost?" I asked reluctantly.

"Fifteen hundred dollars. I know it sounds like a lot, but you really need to consider this, especially since you have only one chance. You want to fertilize as many eggs as possible."

I felt like I was in over my head, but there was no turning back. I agreed to the procedure and then called to tell Mark. I tried to find the humor in all this. "Hey, honey, have you ever wondered why you never knocked up any of your previous girlfriends?"

"What?"

"Well, it's not due to your great skill at the ole pull-out method. I just learned that you have slow hammerhead sperm."

"I have what?"

I explained the call from the nurse and the extra procedure we needed. I told him that basically, the doctor was going to put the sperm into the egg instead of letting the sperm swim to the egg and penetrate it on its own.

"What's the cost?"

"Don't worry. I've got it all under control," I lied.

Mark was stressed about the debt piling up around us. I chose to ignore it and make light of the situation instead. Our roles and dispositions were switching. Usually, I was the serious one and Mark was the joker, but these days everything was upside down.

Janis flew in for the weekend. She wanted to take my mind off the dreadful reality that was becoming my life. We acted like nothing was wrong, as if I didn't have a care in the world. Friday we shopped all day and watched movies in the evening. She and I stayed up all night while she shared the juicy details of her love life and the latest gossip from Miami. It was great to get lost in someone else's life.

On Saturday we got dolled up just like it was another night in South Beach. Club hopping wasn't quite the same in Memphis, but we were ready to take on the town. Mark was a great sport and went along. In the club, he hung back, letting us have our ladies night out. The music pumped loudly while the lights blinked to the beat. We both let loose, dancing up a storm until we could barely walk.

For the next twelve days, I went back and forth to the clinic for blood draws and ultrasounds. After each visit I would receive a call at 4:00 giving me dosing instructions for my nightly injection. My stomach looked like a war zone from all the shots. On the eleventh day, June 7, the nurse called to tell me I was ready for the final shot. She gave me specific instructions to give myself the last dose at 9:00 p.m. The egg retrieval was scheduled for June 9.

That morning, Mark and I waited in a small room. I was in my favorite hospital attire, sitting on a table, all prepped for the procedure. We were just waiting for the doctor. A nice lady with short red hair came in with an incubator and introduced herself as the embryologist. Then a tall Asian man in a white coat entered the room. He introduced himself as Dr. E. and said he'd be performing the procedure.

"Oh, no," I said, "Dr. K. is doing my procedure. I have cancer." The panic was obvious in my voice. "I don't have a cervix anymore because of a radical trachelectomy."

"Calm down. Dr. K. and I have reviewed your unique case. I've already performed an egg retrieval on a patient who had undergone a radical trachelectomy. Dr. K. has not."

I relaxed. Dr, E. spent a few minutes reviewing what steps would be taken once I was put to sleep. I could tell he wanted to make me feel as comfortable with him as possible, and it worked. Mark kissed me on the forehead before leaving the room to go do his part—masturbate into a cup.

I awoke to find Mark by my side. He told me the procedure was a success. Dr. E. was able to retrieve nine eggs from my right ovary. The left ovary hadn't produced any eggs. Everyone was excited about the number of eggs retrieved, which made me feel good about my decision to have the procedure. A nurse gave me instructions to care for myself over the next few days. The lab would call to confirm fertilization within the next twenty-four hours.

I crawled into bed as soon as we arrived home. I felt sick from the anesthesia and wanted to sleep it off. The next morning the redheaded embryologist called. Seven of the nine eggs were mature and two were discarded. All seven were fertilized. My embryos were frozen on day one of life. I was so relieved.

With that call, I crossed fertility off my to-do list. I was a mother—well sort of. It probably should have felt like a momentous occasion, but I was so focused on surviving, on moving forward, that I couldn't really process my feelings. It felt more like an insurance policy, as if I had taken my most precious jewelry and put it in a box for safekeeping.

To add to my confusion, my work situation was becoming more complex by the day. The weekend before the egg retrieval, I had received word that the district manager I was covering for had died. *Would I die too?* I pushed the thought out of my head.

The truth was, I didn't have time for fear. I was juggling doctor appointments, emotional turmoil, and wedding plans while attempting to provide solid leadership (and now grief counseling) to my subordinates.

The following Monday, just two days before we left for Jamaica, my boss called with good news. "I'd like to thank you for your exceptional leadership during this difficult time. I'm aware of your interest in the position out west, but I'd like you to consider staying here in Memphis." He needed to fill the job left vacant by the district manager's passing. "I believe you've proven you're the best person for the job."

We met at a Starbucks to discuss the details, and I accepted the position. It paid more money than I was making at the moment and I didn't have to move. Both were perks, especially given my medical condition. After my coffee meeting, I picked up our mail. I sat in the car flipping through the envelopes and stopped at a large manila envelope with Fertility Clinic written on the outside. I ripped into it and found a black and white photo of seven translucent circles, titled *Maybe Babies, frozen zygotes on day one.* Included was a handwritten note wishing me luck in my cancer battle. A tear fell from my eye as I took my first look at my future children—my Maybe Babies.

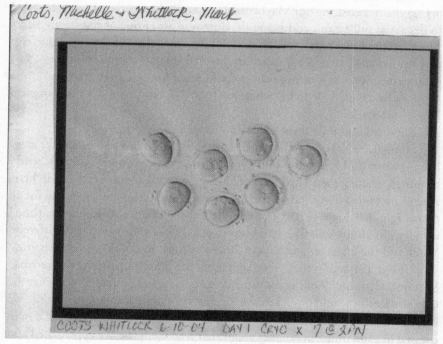

My Maybe Babies; embryos on day 1

Jamaican Wedding

June 2004

Paradise, here we come!

Mark and I hurried around the house early Wednesday morning, exactly one week after creating our Maybe Babies. Our flight to Atlanta was scheduled to depart at 6:00 a.m., and being on time was never one of my strong suits. Mark, on the other hand, prides himself on punctuality. He grabbed my bags and loaded the car while I raced around tending to last-minute items. His calm demeanor was wearing thin. I could sense his agitation growing.

Finally he said, "Michi, whatever it is, I'll buy it for you in Jamaica. Please, can we go?"

I nodded and pulled the front door closed.

Hours later, we stepped off the plane, grateful to be in paradise, far away from doctors and hospital rooms. We followed the crowd into the hot, stuffy terminal, where we searched for our luggage. I recalled my previous trip here, when I had missed my connecting plane and gotten stuck in the States for an extra night. My luggage had arrived in Jamaica without me, and by the time I retrieved it, all my toiletries had been stolen. Luckily, this time was different. We found the luggage, and I was relieved to find that nothing was missing.

Unlike airports in the States, signage at the Jamaican airport was terrible. We strolled around looking for our ride. Our travel agent had told us that the Couples Resort would provide a shuttle, but we had no idea how to find it. We looked around in all directions, hoping for a clue. Then Mark spotted a man dressed in a tan uniform holding a sign that read Couples. We approached and gave the man our bags. He led us into a small room with comfortable chairs and offered us a cool drink. Mark chose Jamaica's finest beer and I had a soda.

"Yah man, it's time to take a ride," another man in a tan uniform said several minutes later, motioning toward our shuttle.

We each grabbed another drink and boarded the shuttle bus along with twelve other couples. Our driver sped through narrow, busy city streets and then down the rough one-lane highways that wound along the ocean. Mark and I sat back and enjoyed the scenery. I tried not to look out the front of the bus; the driver scared me as we zoomed along. The shuttle stopped at several resorts, scooping up passengers along the way.

How ironic would it be if, after all of this, I were to die on some road in Jamaica?

We did arrive at our resort in one piece and walked up the few stairs into the open-air lobby. I felt instantly transported to paradise. The wicker furniture was a light oak color with vibrant red cushions, and sunlight filled the room. A gentleman greeted us with a tray of cool hand towels. We gladly took them and wiped down our hands, faces, and necks, sweaty from our travel. The pool out behind the lobby looked very tempting.

We sat with several other couples, waiting for our room assignments. I recognized a man and a woman from our flight, sitting across from us. He was older with a thick, dark mustache, balding on top but still holding onto his gray hair along the sides and back. His wife appeared younger than him by ten years or more, with her light hair and a colorful skirt. We all introduced ourselves. The age gap between us disappeared as we chatted. Jeff and Sara were from Iowa and had come to Jamaica for a few days of relaxation. We shared the details of our impending wedding. A minute later, a bellhop grabbed our luggage and led us to the honeymoon suite.

Our room was on the second floor. The entryway, long and narrow, opened onto a large room with tiled floors. Two sets of sliding glass doors led out onto a lovely patio with a hammock hanging in the corner. The room was colorful with red molding, green curtains pulled back allowing the bright sunlight in, a canary yellow bedspread, and a multi-colored wall tapestry. It even had a minibar, a whirlpool bath and a separate shower, and a lounging couch. I ran through the room like a five-year-old and jumped on the bed. It was perfect and full of life—just what I needed.

It was mid afternoon and the sun was still high, so we changed into our swimsuits and headed for the beach. We had only to descend a short flight of stairs and turn the corner before sinking our toes into the white sand beach. Now this was living!

We strolled down near the water's edge and dropped our towels on two empty white plastic chairs. "Let's go for a walk and explore," I suggested, tugging on Mark's hand. We walked across the moist sand while the waves broke against our legs. We could see that the beach went on for miles, so we eventually turned back toward our resort. Outside our building we discovered a bocce ball court.

"I love this game!" Mark said. "Will you play with me?"

I wrinkled my nose. "What is it?"

"I learned to play in Italy. It's called bocce."

Mark explained the rules and the objective, and I agreed to give it a try.

We played several games, tossing our balls repeatedly. I even won a game or two. Between the gorgeous sunshine and the opportunity to act like a kid for the first time in months, I found myself enjoying bocce more than I imagined.

When we noticed Jeff and Sara, the couple from the plane, approaching, Mark asked if they wanted to play. We explained the rules and paired off, couple against couple. My competitive nature came out in full force. After another hour, I noticed Mark's skin starting to turn pink and suggested we retreat to our room. Before we left, Sara suggested we all have dinner together. We agreed to meet in the main dining hall at seven.

Mark and I dressed for dinner, but even such a simple act represented the different places we were in mentally. He was looking for a laugh, relaxed and almost carefree. He chose his favorite dark jeans and a red button-down shirt. Two patches decorated the shirt. One read ICEE—you know, the polar bear slush drink you find at the local gas station—and the other was the name Otis, for the town drunk from *The Andy Griffith Show*. Mark has an odd sense of humor, and he thought the shirt was a hoot. I wore a casual, fitted denim dress that highlighted my curves, and three-inch heels to draw attention to my tanned legs. I needed to feel sexy and desirable and to project that image to others. They didn't know I was damaged on the inside. Only Mark knew that beneath the pretty facade, cancer loomed. Unconsciously, I was trying to convince myself I was still worthy of love—Mark's love.

Mark (wearing his famous ICEE shirt) and me in Jamaica

Mark and I arrived at the restaurant promptly at seven. Dinner was served buffet style, featuring an enormous selection of meat, fish, fruit, and sweets. The waiter kept our wineglasses full during dinner, and conversation between the four of us flowed. Jeff, we learned, was a widower. I bluntly asked how his wife had died. I knew it was rude, but I couldn't resist.

"She died young, of cancer, and I raised my girls alone until I met Sara," he responded.

Cancer. Died. Left alone. Was that how our story was going to end? Was I setting up Mark for heartache? I knew it was crazy to think like that, but I couldn't help it. I smiled and pretended to hear the rest of the conversation, but I couldn't quiet the fears in my head.

After dinner, we moved from the restaurant to the bar. The lights were on in the pool and the water was clear and inviting. We ordered another round and continued talking. Mark shared our story, my cancer and our wedding plans. I listened to him talk, amazed at his overall optimism. His voice held not a drop of fear. He told our story as if something was broken and needed to be fixed, simple as that. Listening to him made me realize that beneath my collected exterior, I was terrified.

Sara and Jeff sat close together, holding hands. They seemed so perfect for each other and so happy. *What were they like before they met?* I wondered. *And what about Jeff's first wife? How had they been together? Was Sara the love of his life? Or had that been his first wife? Was our meeting them just a coincidence, or was this a foreshadowing of how our life would turn out? Would Mark be sitting here someday with his new wife long after I was gone, taken by cancer?*

"Michi, honey, are you okay?"

"Yes, yes. Why do you ask?"

"We asked if you wanted another drink and you didn't answer," Mark said. "Plus, your face is white, like you just saw a ghost."

"A drink, yes, please. I could use one of those. No ghost here. Just a bit of jet lag. Sorry I tuned out."

After finishing my glass of wine, I thanked everyone for a lovely evening and excused myself. Mark took my lead and followed me to the room. I thought about sharing my fears but held back. The harsh reality was, this might not end well for me. I didn't want to scare Mark or ruin our wedding, so I said nothing.

The next morning was another adventure. We woke up early and walked along the beach. We had heard that the water activities filled up fast, so we stopped at the water sports shack. The list of possible activities was overwhelming: water skiing, kayaking, surfing, paddle boat rentals, and day trips to other parts of the island.

"There's a catamaran excursion today," Mark said. "Interested?"

"Sure. Let's do it."

We signed up for 3:00 p.m. and then headed to the wedding planner's office to verify all the arrangements. The basic ceremony was included with our stay, but the resort offered several upgrades at an additional charge. Mark and I agreed to no frills and chose flowers from the complimentary list. I wanted something simple and unique to the island, so I selected a native pink flower that matched the embroidery on my dress. The one item we were willing to shell out a bit of cash for was the upgraded package for pictures, including a DVD. Since we hadn't invited anyone else, it would be the perfect way to share the ceremony with our friends and family back home. We received tickets for a thirty-minute couple's massage as well. We scheduled that for Friday morning—the perfect start for our wedding day.

Later we threw on shorts and T-shirts so we could grab a bite to eat. As fate would have it, we ran into Jeff and Sara on our way to lunch. Once again we sat together and talked. Although we seemed an unlikely foursome, we were starting to feel like old pals.

When it was time for our afternoon excursion, we joined the crowd gathered at the water sports shack. In the distance, a catamaran steer toward us. It stopped about twenty yards from the beach and dropped anchor. The couples waded out to it, holding bags, cameras, and towels high above their heads. The crew let down a ladder, and each person climbed aboard one at a time. Reggae blared over the stereo as we settled ourselves. The captain introduced himself and his mates before announcing in his thick Jamaican accent, "The bar is now open. Rum punch for everyone!"

The boat sailed through the water, past the diverse shoreline of the island. I closed my eyes, enjoying the wind across my face and through my hair. Finally the boat glided to a stop.

"Here we are," the captain announced over the speaker. "Rick's Café, famous for the best sunsets in Negril. It sits on top of a forty-foot cliff with only one way up and one way down. Everyone overboard!"

People put down their bags and started leaping into the crystal water. I hesitated. I couldn't see the way up to the café; just a cave where the water rushed in and crashed against the rocks. Mark urged me to jump. I took a deep breath, held my nose, and jumped. The water was cool and refreshing. I resorted to the old-fashioned dog paddle to keep my head above water, and Mark and I followed the others into the cave. There we climbed single file out of the water and onto a rusted, slimy ladder. The narrow passage continued upward, alternating between wet rock steps covered in algae and the rickety ladder. At the top we stepped out into the fresh air and the open-air bar. There weren't many customers there; the catamaran passengers filled up the joint. I took a deep breath, glad to be out of the cave. Some fellow passengers headed straight for the bar and grabbed a drink, while others jumped one at a time off the forty-foot cliff. I did neither. I inched my way near the edge and watched as others plunged into the water. *No way!* I thought. *I can't make that jump. These people have lost their minds.* I stepped back.

Mark was at the bar enjoying a beer. He finished the drink and walked over to the cliff, getting ready to jump. "You're right behind me, right, baby?" he asked. I nodded yes, but I knew I was lying. I wanted to be right behind him, but I was consumed by terror. He let out a cry of joy as he cut through the sky. I watched as he hit the water feet first, torpedoed toward the bottom, and then surfaced, hooting and hollering. He called to me that it was my turn, but I stood there frozen. I couldn't make myself do it. My logical mind knew it was possible to jump and survive—I'd just watched more than twenty people do it and live to tell about it—but my instincts urged me to flee. I shook my head and stepped back again. Mark climbed back up and tried to reason with me. I told him to jump again and not worry about me. He asked me to promise I'd be behind him this time. I nodded. He kissed me and waited in line for his turn. Within minutes he jumped again.

"Last call," came a voice from the boat's loudspeaker. "Everyone at the bar needs to make their way back to the catamaran. We sail in ten minutes."

My stomach sank. I had to do something. The last people made the jump, until it was down to two of us: another scared young woman and me. She started forward and pulled back. The crowd on the boat screamed for her to jump. She was white as a ghost, and I could see the fear on her face. She glanced at me and turned around, heading for the narrow passage down into the cave. I stood on the edge of the cliff, totally alone. Looking down, I could see the rocks below the water's surface. I analyzed the terrain. *The rocks are deeper than you could go. They won't hurt you.*

The logical part of my mind tried to soothe the terrified side, but my heart raced anyway. I flashed back on the recent events in my life. Ever since my cancer had returned, every decision I had made was like leaping off a cliff into the unknown. Suddenly I understood: jumping represented my spirit, my willingness to trust in the outcome. It was an act of total faith. This split second meant life or death; fighting the cancer or giving in. I closed my eyes and leaped.

Adrenaline surged through me. The fall was thrilling and terrifying. I took a deep breath as my feet plunged into the cool water, accidentally swallowing the salty water. I feverishly kicked my feet and waved my hands, sure I was drowning. Panicked, I broke the water's surface, choking. The crowd cheered for me as I swam toward the boat. I felt exhilarated from the rush. I had made the jump and survived!

Later that night, during dinner, Sara said, "I know we just met, but we feel so close to you both. May we come to your wedding?"

"Of course, we'd love for you to come," I said. "You'll be our only guests."

"I can come by and help you get ready, if you like?" she added.

"Great!" I said.

Mark and I spent the early part of our wedding day getting massages and lounging on the beach beneath the bright glow of the sun. I awoke from a short catnap and glanced at my watch. It was 2:30! Sara would be there arriving at our room in less than an hour.

"Let's go," I said to Mark. "I've got to shower." I grabbed my things and raced toward our room. Mark urged me to calm down, even though he knew there was no talking sense into me at a time like this.

I showered quickly and applied my makeup in my usual methodical way. Singing along with his Frank Sinatra CD, Mark calmly got dressed. He slipped into the white linen pants and a white tank undershirt. His shoulders bulged out of the tank. He looked so sexy, I grabbed the camera and took a few shots. He completed his look with the white linen shirt I had bought him. He left the top few buttons open, exposing his chest. As usual, he was ready way before me, causing me to stress more.

I couldn't get my hair the way I wanted it. I fussed with it as my patience waned. Mark advised me to get dressed and let Sara help me with my hair when she got there. I agreed and slipped the dress on, and was immediately overcome with emotion. *This is it. We're really getting married.*

At the sound of knocks, Mark opened the door. "You're just in time," he said to Sara. He directed her to the corner of the room where I was still struggling with my hair.

"Let me," she said. "I have a daughter, after all. I think I can manage."

I sat down and Sara went to work, pulling back the front pieces and securing them with bobby pins. She carefully affixed my veil on top of my head.

"There, just right! Take a look."

I looked up and smiled at her in the mirror. *Perfect.*

Mark, Sara, and I met the wedding planner in the lobby and followed her down a path to a small section of beach. One big, beautiful tree stood there with low hanging branches. Our minister, Keith, whom we had never met before, was waiting for us with Jeff. Waves lapped the shore while a large ship and a few Jet Skiers bobbed in the distance. The sky was bright blue and full of fluffy white clouds that looked like giant cotton balls. On the edge of the path, just before the sand, was a small boom box. Mark placed our Frank Sinatra CD in it, turned it on, and joined Minister Keith on the beach. I walked slowly toward him, conscious of the white sand between my toes. Jeff stopped the music when I reached Mark.

Mark and me moments before our ceremony

The sun was still high in the sky, and the warm rays kissed my cheeks. Mark and I faced each other. Minister Keith slowly read our vows, which I had sent him. Mark looked stoic while I squinted, trying to keep the sun out of my eyes. Minister Keith stumbled over several words; obviously, this was his first time reading the vows.

I had planned so carefully, sending him the vows ahead of time to prevent this from happening. My eyes opened wide as I looked at Mark. Without even speaking, he calmed me down, urging me to go with the flow and enjoy the moment. While Minister Keith continued fumbling over the words, Mark mouthed, "I love you. You are so beautiful." I quietly laughed and held his eyes with mine.

"Now you may kiss!" Minister Keith announced. We both stepped forward and our lips met. Mark lifted me off the sand and spun me around as I laughed. Jeff and Sara clapped and cheered.

Our brief honeymoon was both relaxing and adventurous. I felt alive and yearned to hold onto that feeling. We spent our days waterskiing, sailing a two-seater catamaran out to a small, uninhabited island, and playing bocce ball and relaxing with Jeff and Sara. Our nights were filled with great food, wine, and swimming. Each night ended with a dip in the hot tub before retiring to our room.

Our first kiss as husband and wife

Our trip was magical, and I dreaded returning to real life, the one full of uncertainty and cancer. On our last afternoon in Jamaica, as Mark napped in the hammock on our balcony, I lay restlessly on our bed. I wanted to push out the fears and insecurities that were creeping back in, but I couldn't. Had I made the right decision? Did I wait too long for the operation? Had the fertility drugs caused the cancer to spread? Would I keep my ovaries? Would Mark still love me after the surgery took my womanhood?

I grabbed my stationery and a pen from the suitcase and began writing:

June 2004
Mark Aaron—
My friend, my love ... how do I begin?

Dreaded Surgery

June 2004

Mark and I returned from paradise late in the evening of June 23. I was still on a high from our wedding and didn't want to face the reality waiting for me back home. I had fought this hysterectomy surgery since I was first diagnosed two and a half years ago, but now I had no choice. I knew the doctors were right: if I wanted to live, this was the only way. Still, I felt defeated, forced down a path I never would have chosen. I also feared that my efforts to preserve my fertility had made the cancer worse. If that was true, I wasn't sure I would be strong enough to deal with it. I wasn't good at needing other people. If I broke for real this time, who would put me back together again? Humpty Dumpty had all the king's men; I had Mark. He was supportive, but this was a whole other ball game. *Could he handle it?* I wondered.

Thursday started off with an early morning pre-op session at Dr. D.'s office. The appointment was relatively simple: a quick review of my medical prognosis and more details on what to expect for the operation. The nurse informed me that I needed to pre-register at the hospital and give blood. She handed me a referral for the blood work and surgery before sending me on my way. I waited until I reached the car to read the paper. It listed the procedures the doctor planned to perform: radical hysterectomy, partial vaginalectomy, lymph node dissection and possible removal. It looked even scarier in writing.

I pulled out of the parking lot and headed toward the hospital. My insurance company had insisted I use a hospital in midtown, thirty minutes from my house. I didn't have the energy to fight with them on this one, but as I drove past two other hospitals to reach the "approved" one, I couldn't help but think how crazy it all was. Insurance was supposed to make a patient's life easier, but it always ended up causing more drama.

I was trying not to let cancer take over my life, but this pre-op business was going to take longer than I had figured. I called my assistant and told her to cancel my morning meeting and push back the early-afternoon conference call I had scheduled with the managers who reported to me.

Hospitals can be such a maze. It took me twenty minutes to find parking and the pre-registration desk. The receptionist didn't look very happy to see me. She handed me clipboard with a stack of paperwork without looking up or even cracking a smile.

Really? I thought. *You think* you *don't want to be here? Imagine how I feel, lady.*

Over an hour and a half later, someone finally called my name. The registration nurse asked a few simple questions and then instructed me to go to the lab. Another long hour passed. Finally, it was my turn. I jumped to my feet and hurried toward the examining room. The nurse drew several vials of blood and thanked me for my time.

It was almost time for my conference call. I dialed in, trying to prepare myself for the questions that would inevitably come. I dreaded telling the managers that I, too, was sick. Their previous supervisor had died less than a month before. I dove in and explained that I had cancer. Everyone was quiet. I didn't even hear the sound of breathing over the line. I assured them that I was going to survive, that I'd be in and out of surgery quickly and back at work in a few weeks. There was nothing to worry about.

Here I go again, I thought, *being strong for everyone else. But I didn't even believe what I was saying. How could they?*

The day before my surgery was like any other Sunday. We slept in, and then Mark made breakfast. The weather was beautiful; the sky was clear and the sun was warming the earth. Mark and I loaded our dogs, George and Charlee, in the truck and headed to the nearby state park. The dogs ran off-leash while we enjoyed the warm sunshine, soft breeze, and each other's company. I wanted every last second I could get outside in the sun, since I knew I'd be trapped indoors for the next few weeks.

The evening was more difficult. My anxiety grew. I was short and snappy with Mark, who tiptoed around, trying not to upset me. I busied myself with packing my hospital bag. I included our wedding announcements, my address book, the letter I had written to Mark in Jamaica, and a few basic essentials. I tried to ignore my fears about the surgery, but it became more difficult as the hours ticked by. By the time we climbed into bed and Mark wrapped his arms around me, I was full of mixed emotions.

My mind replayed the word written on the doctor's orders: vaginalectomy. *He's going to cut out more of my vagina! This can't be happening. Not only will I be infertile, I'll be missing a large section of my vagina. Will I ever have sex again? Will I enjoy it? Will Mark still want me when he realizes all I've lost?*

I lay there, torn between initiating a last roll in the hay with my loving, handsome husband or curling up in a ball and giving in to my fear. I wanted to feel him one last time before the scalpel changed me forever, but I just couldn't stop the thoughts racing through my head. Mark fell asleep, and I tossed and turned all night.

My sister and mother had recently moved to Memphis so they accompanied Mark and me to the hospital. It was still dark outside when we pulled into the parking lot. Once inside, I was immediately taken to a small staging area to prep for surgery. The nurse called me Ms. Coots. I couldn't wait to correct her.

"It's Mrs. Whitlock. I got married last week but haven't changed my insurance card yet."

"I'm just reading what the chart says, honey," she snapped. *Rude.* She checked my fingernails to make sure they were free of nail polish. Then she instructed me to remove all jewelry and hairclips. I was only wearing my wedding band. The diamond was at home safe and sound. I reluctantly slid the band off my finger and placed it on Mark's pinky finger.

"Promise you'll wear it until I wake from surgery and you return it to my finger." He nodded in agreement. "No, say it," I insisted.

He smiled and said, "I'll wear it until you wake from surgery and I'll return it to your finger."

Dr. D. came in and greeted me. He reviewed the procedure one last time and mentioned removing both ovaries. I gaped at him. "What? Both ovaries?"

Mark and I reminded him of the agreement he had made with us to biopsy the ovaries during surgery and call Mark with the results. Then he and Mark would decide together what stayed and what would be removed.

"Ah yes. Mark, give me your number." Dr. D. pulled out his Blackberry and typed it in. "I'll call you from the OR, so stay by the phone." He turned to me. "See you in a few." Then he walked out.

My mom and sister were crying. Lori leaned over and kissed my head. Mark wrapped his arms around me, trying to hold back his tears. His eyes were bloodshot. "I love you, baby—more than you know."

"I love you too, crazy," I said, touching his cheek. Suddenly, I remembered the letter. "Mark, reach into my bag and grab the white envelope. It's a note for you. Promise you won't open it until I'm in surgery. You have to wait at least thirty minutes after I am wheeled away. *Promise!*"

"I promise. See you soon!" Tears rolled down Mark's cheeks as he and my family were escorted to a waiting room.

An orderly wheeled me off, through a set of double doors and down a long corridor. The air was cooler in the hallway, and a chill set in. We stopped in another staging area. The last thing I recalled was the anesthesiologist injecting a shot in my IV line and telling me I'd be very sleepy soon. I closed my eyes and thought about the letter I'd just given Mark:

June 2004
Mark Aaron—
My friend, my love … how do I begin?
As you read this letter I am in an induced sleep somewhere else in this building. While the doctor does what he must, you may have to make some tough decisions as I slumber. I hope all goes well and I'm in and out, no problem, man. But if not, know I trust you to make the right decisions to bring me back to you.

If given the choice, save both ovaries. If only one, save the right. The left is no good; it didn't produce any eggs during our retrieval. I hope that is the only choice you have to make. I love you with all my heart, soul, body, and mind. You are a gift to me, and to all those who are lucky enough to know you. I'll dream of your laughter and our alone time, the secret moments only we know about.

You keep these things in your head too. Our love will pull me through this so we can have many, many, many more years. I send you one thousand kisses, double the hugs and strong embraces….

I woke in my hospital room, groggy and in full-body, gut-wrenching pain. My hand gripped a small button connected directly to a morphine pump. I don't know how I knew what it was, but I did. "I need more medicine," I said while repeatedly pressing down on the button. Mark rushed to my bedside. "I need more drugs, the pain is unbearable," I said, tears drenching my face and hair. I turned my head toward him. "My ovaries?" I mumbled.

He smiled, rubbing my head and wiping away my tears. "We kept one," he said.

"Thank you," I whispered, and closed my eyes, drifting back into my medicated haze.

The first twenty hours were fuzzy at best. I alternated between begging for painkillers, throwing up, and occasionally sleeping. After each dose of medication kicked in, I drifted off for a while before the agonizing pain woke me and started the cycle again.

I was shocked the next day when my morphine pump was removed and I was placed on pain pills. A television and a round clock hung on the wall in front of my bed. I filled the time staring at the clock, watching the minutes tick by, anxiously waiting for my next round of painkillers. I was having flashback to how I felt after the RVT; once again, nothing seemed to take the edge off my pain.

I was also conscious enough to realize I had a catheter in place. I didn't like the way it felt and I wanted the nurse to remove it immediately. She agreed to remove it, but in exchange, I had to prove I was able to urinate on my own. A small potty was placed over the regular toilet seat, designed to catch my urine so the nurse could measure and document the amount of output from my body. It made me feel like a three-year-old and I hated it, but the catheter was worse. I shuffled to the bathroom and sat there for twenty minutes until I was able to pee. I would have sat there all day if I had to. No way was she putting that thing back in!

Mark and my mom made sure someone was with me at all times. Mom took the day shift and Mark spent the night with me. During those evening hours he told me about what had happened during my surgery, how he had kept watch over his phone in anticipation of the call from Dr. D.

"Waiting for that call made it the longest day of my life. I felt totally helpless," Mark said, stroking my head. When his cell phone finally did ring, Dr. D strongly recommended removing both ovaries. While he couldn't say for sure that they were cancerous, they had suspicious marks on them. He told Mark that removing them would give me the best shot at survival.

"I knew you felt strongly about keeping at least one ovary." Mark said. "I told the doctor that since the right one appeared abnormal, that he should remove it but keep the left. I know the left ovary didn't produce any eggs but I wanted to honor your wishes." His eyes searched mine, looking for my reaction. "After I hung up I couldn't stop pacing." He wiped a tear from his face. "What if I had made the wrong choice? What if that one decision that I thought I was making out of love for you, what if it actually caused you to suffer even more down the road?"

My heart ached for him. I couldn't help but think how ironic it was that despite all of the scans and imaging and tests and cutting-edge technology available, so many of our toughest decisions had come down to gut instinct and blind faith. I squeezed his hand and assured him that he had made the right choice, the one I would have made.

Each morning, a resident stopped by and reviewed my condition to address any concerns I had. On day two, Dr. D. stopped in. He politely ordered me to start walking a bit. "It will help decrease the risk of blood clots forming in your legs," he explained. Then he removed my dressings and examined the incision. I couldn't resist the urge to know exactly what it looked like, although I was scared at what I might see. I glanced down and tears poured out of my eyes. My fears were confirmed—it was ugly, extending from hip bone to hip bone. *My pretty tummy is gone forever. Will Mark ever find me sexy again?* I turned away while Dr. D. covered it back up. He handed me a tissue and smiled gently.

He didn't have any news on the pathology report, which would give us a clue as to the extent of the cancer. "It can take several days," he told me.

It was just a waiting game now.

There I was in bed with nothing but time on my hands. I dreaded the thought of walking around. I imagined swinging my legs over the edge of the bed, standing up, and stepping forward. The mere thought intensified the pain. I told myself I'd do it after my next dose of painkillers.

The next dose of meds finally came. When I was sure the pills had taken effect, I called my mother over for assistance. She helped me climb out of bed, very carefully. The pain was worse than I'd imagined. I stood holding onto my mom and the IV pole. Taking a deep breath, I searched for the emotional strength to take my first step. I'm still not sure how I managed it, but slowly I walked out of the room and down the hall. I pushed myself to the end of the hall before retreating back to my room. I sat on the edge of the bed, panting to help control the shooting pain.

My desire to regain control of my life trumped everything else. I forced myself to repeat that walk two more times that day. The pain was unreal. Tears rolled down my cheeks with each step, but I pushed forward, determined to make it.

The hospital's stale air was like a thick film coating my skin. I felt dirty and disgusting. I wanted—no, desperately needed—a shower. I had already mastered peeing and walking; it was time to up the ante.

I was determined, yet hesitant, to move again. Pain radiated throughout my body. Sections of my upper and outer thighs were the only areas where I felt some relief. They were totally numb because the nerves had been cut during the surgery. Dr. D. had warned me that this numbness was a potential side effect—and it was the first in a long line I'd come to know during the next several months.

I waited to take a shower until the nurse brought my next dose. My mom urged me not to, telling me I was too drugged and it wasn't safe. But true to form, I exerted my stubborn will and insisted on bathing. She stayed close to me, afraid I might lose my balance and fall as I pushed the IV pole down the hall. The shower was in a recessed cubby in the hallway. Just a concrete box with curtains, it had no door. My mom turned on the water and helped me out of my hospital gown. I stepped into the shower, carefully dragging along my IV line. The warm water kissed my naked skin, reminding me how grateful I was to be alive.

Freshly showered, I geared up for my next mission: getting the hell out of the hospital. Another resident stopped by to check on me in the early afternoon. I pleaded to go home, telling her I just wanted to crawl into my own bed. Her response surprised me. "Have you had a bowel movement yet?"

"No, why?"

"It's important before you're released that we know you have normal bowel function after such extensive abdominal surgery. May I examine you?"

She listened to my heart and lungs and then gently pressed on my abdomen. I flinched but tried to hide the pain. She took a peek at the incision and asked a few more questions, and then glanced at the clock. "Maybe you can go home. It's still early in the day. But you'll need to have a bowel movement first. Pain medicine can cause constipation." She wrote an order for stool softeners and said she'd be back later to check on my progress.

My fighting spirit sank after she left the room. *How was I going to will a poop into existence?* I wondered.

I was just too tired and ready to give in to my growing pain. The nurse brought another dose of meds, and I took them without hesitation. As the drugs kicked in, I drifted off to sleep.

Later, the resident poked her head in. "Any movement yet?"

"No!"

"I'm sorry, but you'll have to stay the night again. I'll see you in the morning."

I turned my head away from the door in total disappointment.

The next day was Friday, my fifth day in the hospital. I wasn't about to be stuck there for the weekend. I climbed out of bed and pulled my IV pole into the bathroom. I didn't feel the urge yet, but I hoped sitting on the toilet would encourage my bowels to do their thing. Forty-five minutes later, nothing had changed. Disappointed, I stumbled back into bed. The resident checked in. After hearing my discouraging news, she gave me a mild laxative. I took it and waited. Nothing happened. I went for my morning stroll and then crawled carefully back into bed, my prison.

Just after lunch, hope arrived in the form of stomach cramps. I moved quickly for someone with a hip-to-hip abdominal incision, heading toward the toilet. I sat and sat and sat. Nothing happened. I was not only in physical pain, but in emotional distress. I eventually gave up and retreated to my bed to wait. About an hour later, my waiting finally paid off. I didn't flush in case I needed proof and pressed the nurse call button. When the nurse arrived, I shared my joy. She wasn't amused. She did agree to let the doctors know, and that was enough for me. I called Mark: "I'm finally coming home!"

Another Crack

July 2004

The car ride home was anything but pleasant. Lori attempted to create a bed for me in the back seat. She even "borrowed" pillows from the hospital. I appreciated her effort, but no amount of padding could make the ride any easier. I held my breath in anticipation as every bump radiated pain through my body.

The house was decorated with balloons and Welcome Home messages. Mark had purchased a stack of movies and all of my favorite foods, but I didn't have any interest in either. I just wanted the pain to stop. That evening, I set up camp on the living room couch. Mark played nurse and ensured I didn't miss a dose of my meds.

When I could no longer hold my eyes open, he urged me to move to our bed. He helped me off the couch and into the bedroom. I headed into the bathroom dressing area and began to remove my clothes.

"What are you doing, Michi?"

"I need to see the scar." I was careful not to call it *my* scar, as I hadn't yet accepted it as a permanent mark on my body.

"Baby, you have seen it. The doctors showed you in the hospital. You don't have to do this tonight. Just come to bed, please."

"No, I need to see the whole picture. I want to stand in the mirror naked and see my reflection." I removed my last article of clothing and stood there, eyes focused on the incision. It curved up at the ends, making it appear slightly u-shaped. *Oh, lovely. It looks like it's smiling at me.*

"Get me a ruler," I said.

"A ruler? That's ridiculous."

"Just get it, now. Please."

Mark reluctantly handed me the ruler. I measured in segments from hip bone to hip bone, being sure to account for every fraction of its curved path.

"Eight inches." I touched it. As I glided my finger across my swollen stomach, the sensation was bizarre and distorted. Some spots were extremely tender while others had no feeling at all. "I'll never wear a bikini again. I'll never be sexy or have a pretty stomach again. I'm ruined!"

"Michi, stop! You need to let your body heal. Of course you're still sexy."

"You have to say that. That's your job." I pulled a T-shirt over my head and crawled into bed, turning away from Mark. If I couldn't bear the sight of my body now, how could he?

Over the next few days, various friends and family arrived, checking on my progress. I felt helpless and depressed lying on the couch, so I insisted on pushing myself. I started weaning myself off the painkillers. They made me feel nauseated, spacey, and out of control. The doctors said it would take me about six weeks to recover. Well, they didn't know me. I was determined to get better in record time.

A few days after I returned home, Andi arrived, ready to take care of me. Every morning I argued with her until she agreed to walk with me around the block. I needed exercise and sunlight to boost my morale. She, like the others, tried to convince me to go easy, but easy was not in my nature. I was moving full steam ahead—or so I thought.

On Thursday, July 8, ten days after my surgery and six long days after my release from the hospital, I had my follow-up appointment. Dr. D. hadn't called with the pathology report yet.

No news is good news, right?

I was nervous but hopeful. Mark offered to accompany me, but I assured him that this was nothing more than a routine post-op appointment. Andi agreed to be my designated driver for the day, and I promised him I would call when we returned. Mark had recently left the restaurant industry and joined a carpet cleaning business. He had started this new job in the midst of my cancer battle; I worried about him missing any more time.

Our wait at the clinic was short. As usual, a student doctor checked on me first and got the details of my recovery. When she asked about my emotional state, I was reticent, not wanting to open up to this stranger. She suggested I try an antidepressant and I snapped at her.

"I'm coping just fine given the circumstances. I'm not depressed!"

She apologized, and I went on to tell her about my mild hot flashes and the lack of feeling across areas of my stomach and upper thighs. I wanted her to have something useful to report to Dr. D., but I was saving my real questions for the expert.

"Michelle, how are you?" Dr. D. asked as he entered the room. He gave me a big hug. "I hear you're experiencing hot flashes. I'll run a test to be sure your remaining ovary is still functioning. Remember, we did remove one ovary, so it may just be a symptom of the reduced estrogen in your body. There are some antidepressants we can use to relieve the symptoms."

"I'm not depressed!"

"You can't use hormone replacement therapy because it could cause your cancer to return. Some antidepressants act on a part of the brain that actually limits or prevents hot flashes. It's a good alternative to hormone therapy. Let's run the test and then make a decision."

When he asked to see the incision, I slid the elastic waistband down on my pants and let him check it out. "You're healing nicely," he said, but then his tone changed. "Now, let's talk about your pathology report."

Oh, no, this is not good news. I held onto the side of the examining table, looking first at him and then at Andi.

"The cancer was worse than initially expected," he said. "It extended through more than 50 percent of the uterine wall." My mouth fell open. "Given its extent and that fact that we're dealing with recurring cancer, I feel we must discuss radiation and chemotherapy as options for you."

"What? No!" I looked over at Andi, who stared at the floor, apparently unable to make eye contact with me. Tears streamed down my face. Dr. D. tried to console me as I sat there in disbelief. I had thought the surgery would be enough.

Before leaving, I agreed to see a radiation oncologist and to think about Dr. D.'s recommended treatment plan. I was too stunned to say no. I couldn't process this latest news. He asked me to return in two weeks and gave me a copy of the pathology report. Andi and I drove home in silence. There was nothing left to say.

I phoned Mark on the way and asked him to meet me at the house. He arrived shortly after Andi and I did. "What's going on, baby? You're scaring me."

"He wants me to have radiation and chemotherapy."

"Why?"

I repeated everything we had learned at the appointment and handed him the pathology report. I looked into his eyes and saw the fear he was trying so desperately to fight back.

Is this my fault? Did I cause the cancer to spread by insisting on waiting for the surgery until after the wedding? Or by taking the hormone drugs to induce ovulation for the egg harvest? Have all my decisions up to this point been wrong?

I would never know. All I could do now was make another choice and hope for the best.

"I'll consider chemo, but I will not have radiation!" I firmly stated to both Mark and Andi. "My grandmother had radiation and it ruined her life. I won't subject myself to it and the subject is not open for discussion." With that, I stood up and left the room.

Decisions

July 2004

The weekend was difficult, but I handled it the best way I knew how—by marching ahead. I went on as if nothing had changed, while everyone else tiptoed around me. I quit taking the pain medicine completely and increased my walks. I started calling work and checking in on things. I desperately needed to feel useful. I was more determined than ever to get well and live my life. There was no time to waste.

Tuesday was Andi's last day with me and Caryn's first. They were passing the torch of responsibility: cheer up Michi.

Caryn was a breath of fresh air. Unlike most people who think about what they are about to say and process the possible reactions of their audience, Caryn spoke with no filter. She had no sense of tact and said whatever was on her mind. I loved that about her. Okay, I loved it most of the time.

I was looking forward to her candid perspective, and she didn't hold back. "What are you wearing?" she said soon after she arrived. "You have cancer—you're not dead. Give me the directions to Target. You need a quick and cheap makeover."

"You're such a bitch!"

"Yes, and you look like hell, darling."

She took me directly to the store. "Super Target and a Starbucks. I love it!" she exclaimed.

We searched the racks for cotton pants that were comfortable yet fashionable. My one requirement was that the waist had to be elastic or have a drawstring. My stomach was still swollen and very sensitive. An hour later we left with a new recovery wardrobe in tow--exactly what I had been needing!

As we drove back to the house, Caryn jumped directly into the heavy stuff. "I know you don't want to talk about it, but that's not reality. Can't we all just go see the radiation oncologist and hear what she has to say? You're not committing to it, just checking out the options."

"I guess the nurse did go ahead and make me an appointment."

"Great! Now that we have that mess settled, let's have some fun!"

At the house, Caryn insisted I take a shower, put on my new clothes, and fix my hair and makeup. She was right; I did feel better. We spend the rest of the day on the couch gossiping, laughing, and watching movies.

Three days later, Friday July 16, was the big day: the appointment with the radiation oncologist. Dr. J. was an older woman and very direct with Mark and me. Since she had already reviewed my case with Dr. D., she merely asked a few questions and then put her cards on the table.

"If you want to survive, you need to have radiation and chemotherapy."

There it was, point-blank. *No sugar at this tea party.* I thought.

I thanked her for her opinion and explained my fear, how my maternal grandmother had also had some sort of gynecologic cancer, and how the radiation had ruined her bladder.

At age twenty-nine, I wasn't just worried about saving my life, but also preserving my quality of life. For me "bladder bag" and "quality of life" didn't fit in the same sentence.

The doctor listened intently. When I finished talking, she acknowledged my fear and explained the risks of the radiation as she saw them. She assured me that the field of oncology and radiation had developed greatly since my grandmother was treated. She felt that the risks today were in no way comparable to the risks in that earlier era.

"So it can't burn a hole in my bladder?" I asked.

"I'm not saying that it couldn't happen, but it's unlikely. There is a greater risk of injury to your bowel, but we'll take proper precautions to minimize that danger." She explained that she was working with the latest research, which studied the maximum amount of radiation any given organ can sustain. This research enabled doctors to administer enough radiation to fight the cancer, but not enough to cause significant damage. "Please consider having the treatment," she urged me.

We thanked her and left. I didn't feel any better. I was emotionally exhausted and stuck between the lesser of two evils: radiation with possible side effects, or no radiation and the likely recurrence of cancer. The choices sucked. Mark filled Caryn in during the ride home while I stared out the window, feeling totally hopeless.

I knew of only one other person who might be able to relate: Kristi, the patient Dr. C. had suggested I call about the embryos. We had spoken a few times back in May, but I didn't really know her. Still, I felt lost and wanted to connect with someone who could understand what I was going through. When we got home, I pulled out her number and called. I reintroduced myself and just started talking. Kristi listened and related to my pain and desperation. She hadn't needed radiation or chemotherapy, but she remembered fearing she might. My unusual friendship with her was my initiation into the sisterhood of cancer, and it taught me the power of sharing with another who has walked before you or after you.

(Another) Health Insurance Nightmare —————

July 2004

Apparently, having recurring cancer and facing the combination of radiation with chemotherapy wasn't stressful enough. When we got home, I grabbed the mail out of the mailbox. Flipping through it, I found the medical bills were piling up. I slit open one envelope, exposing a balance due of $2,048. I tore into another to find another debt—this one for $1,233—not covered by the insurance company. My shoulders slumped under the weight of the financial responsibility.

I dropped the bills on the kitchen counter and sank onto the couch. Why wasn't the insurance company paying? I pulled a blanket over my head. I had no idea how I was going to pay these bills. We were already living paycheck to paycheck. I had spent all our available cash—and then some—on our embryos.

With that realization, fear set in. *What if the treatment makes me too sick to work?* We couldn't survive without my income. Grandma had already helped me with some of the cost for my embryos. I didn't have anyone else to turn to.

The next day another bill arrived, a charge from the pathology lab for several thousand dollars. I called their billing office and then waited on hold for ten minutes. By the time a customer service representative greeted me, I was fuming. I explained my case, insisting the bill was wrong and that she needed to submit it to my insurance company.

"Your insurance company declined," she said politely, "claiming you haven't met your deductible yet. I'm afraid you are responsible for this bill."

"But I have met my deductible!"

"I'm sorry. You'll have to talk to your insurance company."

I slammed down the phone and flipped through the bills on the counter, looking for the latest insurance statement. Surely someone had made a mistake.

I called the insurance company and told their representative about the mix-up with the pathology bill. I waited patiently while she reviewed my account, only to be told the bill was correct. She explained that the pathology lab wasn't contracted with the insurance company and therefore was considered an out-of-network provider.

"How can that be?" I exclaimed. "It's the hospital's lab! Let me get this clear. I called and set up my surgery through you, my insurance company, to be sure it would be covered. You told me where to have it and I listened. I was unconscious on the operating table when the organs the surgeon removed from me were taken to the approved hospital's lab—but it's not covered? Something's very wrong with this picture!"

"I'm sorry, ma'am, but it works that way sometimes."

I felt the pressure building behind my eyes as I argued with this woman. I couldn't believe what she was telling me or how she was treating me. Was I really supposed to wake up midsurgery and insist that my organs go to another lab, one outside the hospital? This had to be a really bad dream.

I filed an appeal, but it was denied. The representative from the pathology lab advised me that I could set up payment installments, but I needed to start paying. I reluctantly agreed to pay $50 a month. I was so mad about the bills, especially the one from the pathology lab, that I told anyone who would listen to me. It gave me a focus other than my illness.

Two weeks later, I received a surprising letter. It was from Janis and her mother, Yvonne. Yvonne had always treated me like a second daughter. I opened the envelope and slid out the get well card, and two slips of paper fell onto the counter. Mark grabbed them: each was a check for $1,000! We looked at each other, frozen with shock. The card simply read:

You shouldn't have to go through this alone—physically, mentally, or financially. We know this isn't much, but we hope it will help.
Love, Janis and Yvonne

That moment of generosity was exactly the attitude adjustment I needed. I woke up the next day with a new outlook. The stress of these bills would not jeopardize my recovery. I would not put a price tag on my life.

I called the billing departments of each of my health-care providers and calmly explained my situation. I thanked them for their medical care and acknowledged it was a difficult position for us both: I needed care and they needed to be paid. I made it clear that they would receive their entire payment from me eventually. In the meantime, I arranged minimum payments that fit my budget. I hung up thinking that I didn't care if it took me the rest of my life to pay them back—at least I was alive!

Heavy Artillery

August to September 2004

I dreaded the start of radiation and chemotherapy. Nearly six weeks after the radical hysterectomy, my body was starting to heal, and now I was about to put it through another round of hell.

Which was better: knowing what to expect or not knowing? I wasn't sure anymore. *Ignorance is bliss,* I finally decided. I usually planned things out and researched all the facts and angles before making any decision, but not this time. The bit I did know about radiation scared the hell out of me. The doctors tried to reassure me, but nothing they said made any difference. The fact was that I had known someone who had suffered permanent damage from radiation, and it was the only thing I could think of.

Chemo was a different story. I didn't personally know anyone who had experienced chemotherapy. I had only seen stories on television and in movies, in which the actors get sick, throw up, and lose their hair. It didn't sound like a walk in the park, but at least the nausea went away and the hair grew back. I was pretty sure I could handle it.

As I pondered losing my hair, Demi Moore's face flashed in my mind. She had shaved off all her hair for that movie *GI Jane,* and yet she was still beautiful. I tried to tell myself I was strong enough to sport a bald head. It was only hair, after all. Right?

In additional to the many doctor appointments and the CAT scan of the past week, I now had semi-permanent pelvic tattoos (marks the radiologist had drawn on me to identify internal organs not to radiate). They looked ridiculous, but those marks were key to me keeping my bladder. They needed to remain visible for the entire treatment period. My anxiety grew while my mind played out a thousand and one endings to my story.

Monday, August 9, marked day one of radiation. I arrived at 8:00 a.m. and settled into the waiting room with the other patients. No one made eye contact; they all read or looked down at the floor. I had drunk a quart of water because I had been told I needed to have a full bladder while receiving the radiation. I really needed to pee and hoped it wouldn't be much longer.

A few minutes later I heard them call "Michelle Whitlock." *Michelle Whitlock.* Even with all of the anxiety swirling inside me, hearing my new name made me smile. I walked to the nurse slowly, still considering the possibility of bolting for the door and never coming back.

"Ready to get started?" she asked in a chipper voice.

"Sure," I said, feeling anything but ready. I walked behind the curtain and waited some more. My bladder was beginning to hurt. I squeezed my muscles tight, trying to hold it in.

A technician led me into the radiation room and instructed me to lie on the table. I unbuttoned my pants and slid them down, exposing my entire pelvic region, midthigh to navel. The machine was placed over my body and a protection plate was slid in place to guard the organs inside the tattooed lines. The protection plate looked like a clear plastic tray with metal blocks in various shapes bolted to it. There was one for each view of my pelvis: front, back, left, and right. The technician checked to make sure the machine was lined up properly and then left the room. I held my breath for a minute or so but didn't feel a thing. The technician returned, changed out the protection plate, and repositioned the machine to another view. He repeated the process until the radiation fired through me from all angles. The entire procedure took less than ten minutes, and it was quick and painless. I left and headed to work.

I repeated this exact process every Tuesday, Wednesday, Thursday, and Friday. The plan was to give me radiation five days a week for five and a half weeks. Saturdays and Sundays were my only days of rest. My first chemotherapy session started the same week as radiation. Chemo was scheduled for Thursdays only for six weeks. It all sounded easy enough.

The chemotherapy may have been only one day a week, but the session lasted seven or eight hours. Mark and I went to the lab, where a nurse placed an IV line in my arm, drew some blood, and then led me to an exam room. Dr. D. entered and reviewed with me what I should expect. He offered me the name and number of another patient, Evelyn. He told me Evelyn was a few years older than I, but she had been through a similar treatment protocol and was willing to share. I took the number and shoved it into my purse.

"I've decided just to shave my head now, instead of waiting for it all to fall out," I declared.

"Don't do that," he said. "You're going to take a drug that shouldn't make you lose your hair."

I was shocked by his response. It had taken awhile to get used to the idea, but I was ready to embrace the baldness. Now Dr. D. was telling me it wouldn't happen. I was confused. Didn't everyone lose their hair during chemo?

I learned that every chemo drug is different, and each can be used alone or in combination, depending on the type of cancer. The drug the doctors had chosen to treat my cancer might cause some thinning, but not total hair loss. On the other hand, it was known to be one of the worst chemo drugs in terms of nausea. The greatest risk I faced was kidney failure, so cutting out caffeine and staying hydrated was crucial during treatment.

Great, I thought. *There goes my one vice: good ole fashioned Coke classic.* I had been raised on classic Coca-Cola and loved drinking it for breakfast, lunch, and dinner. I loved it so much, that Mark usually brought me a Coke in bed before work. Now cancer was taking that away too. I knew that in the big scheme of things, a can of Coke was not a big deal, but it felt like a symbol for every way my life was being turned inside out.

Eventually, Mark and I were led into the chemo room. It was bright, surrounded by windows, and filled with blue leather reclining chairs. A nurse showed me to a chair, gave me a blanket, and hooked up my first bag of fluids. She explained that this bag was saline to hydrate me. Then I would get a bag of steroids and antinausea medication, which would take another hour. Finally, she would administer the chemo drugs, followed by another bag of saline fluids, again for hydration. Each of those bags would take close to two hours. "Get comfortable, sweetie," she said with a smile. "You're gonna be here all day."

I settled in and flipped open my laptop. I might not be able to go to work, but they couldn't stop me from bringing work to the chemo room. I was determined to keep life as normal as possible. With my cell phone and laptop charged, I had plenty to do. The bright side was that I could count it as an office day, so I didn't have to use sick leave. Mark stayed with me the entire time as well.

After the chemo was done, I was given steroid pills and additional anti-nausea medication. The nurse reminded me to drink lots of fluids. "Hydration is the key," she repeated, like a mantra.

For the first two days, I felt pretty good about my decision to have chemo and radiation—until the side effects kicked in. I woke up Saturday and felt like I had run a marathon. I was thirsty, and my eyes felt too heavy to hold open. It felt so surreal. I had no motivation. I didn't want to get out of bed or even eat.

Mark entered the room. "Are you up, sleepyhead? I've got a big, tall glass of juice here." I cracked my eyes open, looked at him, and rolled over. "You have to force fluids. Just take a sip. Please."

Reaching for the glass took all my strength and will. Mark smiled and asked if I was hungry.

"No. I'll just lie here a bit." I closed my eyes and tried to conjure up images of food, but nothing appealed to me. Every time I thought of eating anything, I wanted to vomit.

"Will you call that other patient and talk to her?" Mark asked. "I'm worried about you."

"Fine. The number is in my purse. Can you please dial it? I can't move."

When Mark handed me the phone, I explained to Evelyn who I was and why I was calling. We didn't know each other and yet instantly we were friends, kindred spirits. Cancer has a funny way of bonding people. I rattled off a list of questions and she answered them all. There were no boundaries. We talked for over an hour, sharing our stories. It was so reassuring to know that someone else understood my pain, emotional and physical. I started to think that everything might be okay.

Unfortunately, it wasn't long before radiation-inspired diarrhea kicked in. I raced back and forth between the bed and the bathroom. While sitting on the toilet during another bout with diarrhea, I noticed that the blond peach fuzz on my stomach and thighs was disappearing. Even my pubic hair looked thinner and lighter. *Oh shit! My hair is falling out after all.* I grabbed a handful of hair on my head and pulled. *Ouch!* That hurt, so okay, my hair was still attached. But what exactly was happening to me?

The second week of treatment was much the same as the first. I arrived for my radiation every morning, Monday through Friday. Dr. W., another radiation oncologist, visited with me for a few minutes on Wednesday to check on my developing symptoms. He sat on his round blue stool in his white jacket, jotting down notes. I complained about the constant diarrhea, my raw behind, and recent hair loss.

"Radiation can cause hair loss in the immediate area being treated," he said. "Not to worry, it will grow back." He handed me another prescription to help with the diarrhea.

I tried to think of the bright side. At least I wouldn't have to shave for a while. But it didn't exactly feel like an even trade.

The second chemo session was exactly as the week before, long and uneventful. I climbed into bed as soon as I got home and passed out. With the exception of my sprints to the bathroom, I didn't move until the next morning.

Friday was tough. I struggled to make my radiation appointment. The fatigue was killing me. Just putting one foot in front of the other was a chore. I wanted to go home and sleep, but I refused to give in. I pushed my way through the day by focusing on the sunny side: I hadn't vomited yet, although I was now prone to gagging.

The weekend was the one time I didn't push myself and didn't pretend I was stronger than I knew I was. I just gave in. Besides, I wanted to be near my new best friend—the toilet. The diarrhea was becoming more than I could handle. The balance between what was going in my body and what was coming out was way off. I could hardly swallow anything solid. I had lost my appetite and developed a metallic taste in my mouth. I established a new house rule: no one could cook around me. The odor of food cooking was sickening.

Whenever I did find a bit of energy, I called Evelyn. She listened intently and let me complain. She had been through this war and knew each and every battle. I never worried she'd get tired of listening to me as I did with my other friends.

After my shower on Monday I stood in front of the mirror and looked at myself. I mean, really looked at myself. My face was sunken and my skin was yellow, except where it was red and burned from radiation. I slowly turned, taking in the view from every angle. I closed my eyes. It couldn't be true. I had to be having a nightmare. I looked again, this time through the sheen of tears. My perfect heart-shaped ass was gone. I had been robbed!

I threw on a towel and headed for the kitchen. Mark was standing in front of the fridge stirring a protein shake for me. As soon as he saw my face, he asked what was wrong.

"My ass is gone! Gone! All my curves are gone! I'm just a bag of bones." I fell into his arms, sobbing.

He held me and rubbed my back. "Oh, baby, don't be silly. You look fine."

"Stop lying. This cancer has taken everything—my uterus, my fertility, my womanhood, my hope, my strength, my perfect tummy, and now even my ass. What will be left of me? I'm drained and I don't have any body parts left to give." I crawled back into bed.

Within minutes, I heard my cell ring. "It's work," Mark yelled. "I'll take a message."

"No, no, give it here." I wiped my eyes and took the phone. This call was exactly what I needed to stop feeling sorry for myself. I had to stay focused and busy, and to feel needed. Work helped me do that. I dressed and headed out for week three of radiation and work.

Hell, as I knew it, began Friday morning of that week. I woke up feeling incredibly ill. I barely made it to the toilet before vomiting. Then I had to sit on the toilet with a trash can in front of me because I had it coming out both ends. Mark called the doctors and reported the severe symptoms. Within an hour he had a new prescription, and my vomiting stopped.

I still felt like a train wreck, gagging and having runny bowels. Mark encouraged me to stay home and rest. "Baby, you can't keep pushing yourself."

I ignored him, unwilling to accept my limitations. I dressed as quickly as my bathroom breaks allowed and went to work anyway. I spent most of the day running for the restroom. I was dreadfully sick and I wasn't fooling anyone. It took me all day to complete a few simple tasks. It finally dawned on me that I wasn't Superwoman. I think I had actually fooled myself into believing I could handle anything. Apparently, I was wrong. I was unraveling.

That night, I walked in the door and fell on the couch. Mark had dinner ready—spaghetti. He had cooked it before I arrived in accordance with my no-cooking-in-my-presence rule. Mark put the food down in front of me. I pushed it away. I hated eating by this point and struggled just to force fluids down my throat.

"Please eat a few bites," he said. "Your body needs fuel to keep fighting." He stared at me with sad eyes. "Please?"

"Fine, I'll try."

I struggled with every bite. I hated the whole thing—the smell, taste, and texture. I practiced an old trick my dad had taught me to get the food down—holding my nose before putting the food in my mouth, so I couldn't really taste it. It was so silly. Here I was at twenty-nine, acting like I was in kindergarten.

When I couldn't force another bite, I asked him to take it out of my sight. I lay back on the couch and flipped through the stations on TV. My stomach was turning and making crazy noises. I started gagging and heaving. I sprang from the couch and ran for the bathroom, my hands over my mouth as I desperately tried to hold it in. I bent down, stuck my face into the toilet, and vomited uncontrollably. Mark was right there, trying to hold my hair back.

I heaved again and felt sudden panic. I waved my arms around. *Help, help, help! I'm choking!* I wanted to scream, but no words came out. Food blocked my throat. I violently thrust my stomach muscles, trying to dislodge the food. Mark didn't get my signals; instead he kept rubbing my back in an attempt to comfort me. I was totally panicked. I couldn't get any air and I genuinely thought I was going to die. I rammed my hand into my mouth and feverishly scooped out partially digested spaghetti. *This can't be it. I will not die face down in the toilet.* I forced my hand deeper into my throat and shoveled out more, freeing my airway. I coughed and choked up the remaining spaghetti as I gasped for air. I collapsed on the floor, frightened, weak, and crying.

Mark called the hospital. Within an hour, I was in the emergency room waiting to be admitted. The resident was concerned about possible kidney failure due to dehydration and thought I should stay the night. Once I was given my own room, Mark and I squeezed into the single bed. I didn't want to be alone. The nurse hooked me up to IV fluids and injected my line with anti-nausea medication. An agonizing pain shot up my arm.

"Damn it! It burns, it burns!" I screamed.

"That's a possible side effect with this medication," she said with a shrug.

"Well, make it stop!" I said, giving her the most evil look I could conjure.

She casually filled a vial with saline and prepared another injection. She might as well have been making a pizza. I know to her it was just another shift, but to me, the whole experience was totally traumatic. *Don't you understand?* I wanted to yell at her. *I almost choked to death! In my bathroom*! Instead I just continued to glare at her while she flushed out my line in an attempt to relieve the burning. It was too little, too late; the damage was done. The vein was dark and puffy halfway up my arm.

In the morning, Dr. D. arrived. I didn't give him time to speak. "I will not do any more chemo. I can't take it," I cried.

He acknowledged the terrible experience, but then reviewed the benefits of continuing treatment. I cried and shook my head. He looked at me in silence for a long moment, probably hoping I'd change my mind.

Finally he said, "Take the next week off of chemo. Come see me Thursday and let's talk then. No decisions have to be made today. You've had a difficult night."

After a few more hours of fluids, I was released. Mark drove straight home. I immediately climbed into my bed and, except for the frequent trips to the bathroom, stayed there until Monday morning.

Monday brought with it another week of radiation. I wanted to bail, but I forced myself to go. I felt terrible, but I knew this course of treatment was my best shot at survival. I tried to focus on the long-term benefits, but found it nearly impossible to push aside the agony.

As I climbed onto the table, the technician asked, "How are you feeling today?"

"All my pubic hair is gone, my skin is painfully sensitive, and the diarrhea never stops. How about you?"

He just smiled, realized I wasn't in the mood for small talk, and jumped right into the radiation. As he left the room, pity was written all over his face, and I hated it. I lay there, thinking about how most twenty-nine-year-old women were either on the career path with their briefcase in hand, or on the mommy track with a baby on one hip and a diaper bag in their hand. Not me. My briefcase now held my spare panties and wet wipes for when I shit my pants in public. Every girl's dream.

I insisted on seeing the radiation oncologist before leaving the building. I complained about the extreme symptoms: constant diarrhea, rectal bleeding, burning pain, and the most fun—incontinence.

He prescribed yet another medicine and gave me all the reasons to continue with this treatment. I only had two a half weeks to go, and he assured me the symptoms would stop as soon as the treatment was over.

Easy for you to say. You try it sometime.

The exhaustion was kicking my butt. It took all I had to climb out of bed and make it into work each day. My boss insisted I cut back my hours. Since I wouldn't put limitations on myself, he'd decided to do it for me. I was already working from home on Mondays and from the chemo room on Thursdays. I'd given up traveling out of town during treatment. Now my boss insisted I work from home on Fridays too.

"You have plenty of administrative things that can be done from the comfort of your own home," he continued. "I don't want a repeat of last week with you in the hospital again."

I reluctantly agreed.

Immediately following radiation on Thursday, I headed for Dr. D.'s office. He asked all the basic follow-up questions, and then suggested I pick up with the chemo again the next week and finish out the last three treatments. He tried to reason with me, citing statistics about five- and ten-year survival rates. As he spoke, reality seeped in. Tears filled my eyes and then overflowed. He stretched his hand out, waving a fluffy white tissue. I grabbed it and he hugged me, once again reminding me why I had chosen him as my surgeon.

When I was calm again, he said, "Tell me what you are feeling. I want to understand."

I shared all my issues. The hot flashes and night sweats, exhaustion, constant nausea and the runs. My newest fear was dying on my toilet either by suffocating on vomit or bleeding to death from my ass.

"I can't bear the thought of entering a bathroom, yet I have no choice. None of the medicine has helped with the pain or symptoms. I find myself screaming, crying, and fleeing from the toilet to the tub, just for some mild relief." More tears poured. I had lost what little sense of modesty I had left. I was emotionally raw and exposed.

"May I examine you?" he asked.

He actually asked for permission, another great character trait. He didn't assume his position automatically gave him the right. That simple request returned to me a sense of dignity and respect—feelings I hadn't felt in quite a while.

The examination uncovered the source of my pain: a long fissure in the rectal tissue. He told me radiation can thin out the skin as it burns both good and bad cells alike. The constant diarrhea and wiping had caused the already sensitive tissue to tear.

"Imagine the worse paper cut you've ever had," he said. "Now imagine having that paper cut in the most sensitive area of your body. No wonder you're in such agony."

He applied numbing Lidocaine with a large Q-tip and gave me a tube to take home.

"One more thing," he said. "The test shows you are in menopause. The radiation has damaged your remaining ovary. I'm sorry."

I fought so hard to hold onto that ovary, all for nothing.

"How about your chemo?" he asked. "Will you please continue?"

I sat there considering my choices, considering the future benefits of today's suffering. I took a deep breath. "I'll start again next week and do the last two sessions. I won't make up today's session. Two more, that's it. Okay?" I looked directly into his eyes without blinking.

He smiled. "That's better than nothing. Go get some rest, and please try to eat more protein. Your body needs it to heal. I know this has been tough; radiation is especially hard on thin people. Keep fighting!"

Mark took me home and tucked me in before returning to work. I had no energy or motivation left. I spent the afternoon in bed, feeling sorry for myself. Mark called after work to tell me he was going to happy hour with this brother. He promised to be home after two drinks. I knew what that meant. Usually when they got together, "two drinks" turned into a late night. I feared tonight would be the same.

"Okay," I said in a tone letting him know it really wasn't.

"Michi, it's two beers. Please don't be like that."

"I said it was fine. Go have fun."

I didn't mean a word of it and he knew it.

I wasn't being fair, but I couldn't help it. After months of trying to be strong and pretending like everything was going to be fine, I couldn't hide the truth: I was miserable, scared, and lonely. I just wanted him home with me. Mark, however, needed to get out and talk with someone in the real world. He needed an escape from my cancer and from playing caretaker. Rationally, I knew he needed this time for himself, but my rational side was no longer in control. I feared he would like it better out there at the bar than home with his cancer-stricken wife. I knew he loved me, but I was so sick and needy. Not much of a turn-on. Mark had always been devoted and faithful, but we hadn't had sex in two and a half months. I was feeling insecure and unattractive, and I was acting crazy.

You're the sick one, not him, I told myself. *He's still a healthy, handsome, sexy man with desires. And you're not meeting any of them.*

Over the years I had heard men joke about their how their sex lives ended when they got married. Mark's really did. I felt bad for him, and I worried about what it might mean for our relationship. I wanted to erase those thoughts, but they kept haunting me. *There will be some pretty girl at the bar. She'll flirt with him and throw herself at him. He loves you, but he's still a man and you aren't putting out,* I worried.

After we hung up, I lay in bed waiting, feeling stupid and vulnerable, hoping he'd really come back after two drinks but bracing myself for the worst. Two hours later, Mark surprised me by walking through the door.

He'd even stopped to rent some movies. I knew he could have stayed at the bar with his brother and all of the pretty girls there who didn't have cancer, but he chose to come home to me. Even at my most broken point, he still wanted to be with me.

Week five was ugly. Mark made arrangements for his mother, Teri, to come and stay with us for the rest of my treatments. His work schedule was filling up fast, and I was getting sicker by the day. I hated all food and my weight was down to a measly 112 pounds. Not a pretty sight.

I was scheduled to meet with my boss on Tuesday morning. It was midyear performance review time, and I hadn't seen him since my promotion back in early June.

I went to radiation as scheduled and returned home to get ready for my meeting. Lori came to help me. Another bad bout of the runs hit and forced me into the bathroom. I was so raw, I couldn't bear the thought of toilet paper on my skin. "Lori!" I shouted. "Please come quickly." I was doubled over crying when she appeared in the doorway. "Run the tub. Please hurry!" As soon as the water was two inches deep, I hobbled from the toilet and into the tub.

I stayed there while she sat on the floor beside me. I felt so helpless. It wasn't long before my stomach turned again. I leapt like a frog out of the tub and hurried back to the toilet. Then back into the tub. I told Lori to call my boss and push my meeting back one hour. "If he asks why, be vague." Just as I thought, he asked a million questions. Lori handled him perfectly and gave few details. He offered to cancel the meeting, but Lori did as I requested and insisted we just move it back. I wanted to be my normal, career-oriented self and I really wanted to make that meeting. My body, on the other hand, didn't care two cents about the meeting, work, or anything else except stopping the agony.

The pain worsened; I couldn't leave the bathroom. Eventually, Lori called back and canceled the meeting. My boss was totally supportive, but I felt like I had hit rock bottom. I had to face the cold, hard truth: cancer had the upper hand and there was nothing I could do about it.

The next morning I rolled over, looked at the clock, and then covered it up. I wasn't getting up, and I wasn't going back to radiation. I couldn't handle another day. I called and informed the doctor of my decision. The nurse suggested I take the day off and return the following day for the last few sessions. She obviously didn't understand what I was saying. I was done and I wasn't coming back. I didn't want to hear about the benefits, how the treatment would save my life. As far as I was concerned, this wasn't living. I was a prisoner to my bathroom and it needed to end.

Teri arrived late that evening. She settled in and went right to work taking care of us. She went grocery shopping and planned meals. Mark broke the news about my no-cooking rule to her. Teri loved to cook and make sure everyone was fed, but she understood and took the news like a champ. She just got to work setting plan B in motion: takeout. She was exactly what we needed—help for me and stress relief for Mark.

After having a day off to clear my head, I was feeling defeated but able to think more rationally. I decided to finish radiation and chemo. I told myself it was just one more week. *I can do anything for a week,* I repeated over and over.

The chemo session went south from the beginning. The nurse searched my arms for a vein so she could start the IV line. I was so dehydrated and thin now. I had been poked and pricked so many times over the last few months, finding a good vein was almost impossible. Finally, she was able to find one on my forearm. She prepped the area. "Take a deep breath."

As soon as the needle hit my arm, the vein rolled away from her. *Oh, not this again,* I thought. *I've been through hell already this week and I'm hanging on by a thread.*

She moved the needle around under my skin, attempting to reach and penetrate the vein. I flinched with pain. "I'm sorry," she said. "Let me get someone else. I don't want to hurt you again."

Moments later another nurse sat before me. "I always get the tough ones around here," he joked. He grabbed both of my arms and pulled them straight out, turning them to side to side. "You are difficult, aren't you?"

"Chemo and radiation will do that to a person," I replied sarcastically.

He tapped on my arm. "Okay, I've got one." He wiped the spot with an alcohol swab and pressed the needle beneath my skin. I pulled back. "Got it," he exclaimed, obviously proud of his accomplishment.

Somebody get this guy this a trophy, I thought sourly. I had lost my sense of humor and it wasn't coming back anytime soon.

An hour into the first bag of fluids, I felt my bowels turn. I closed my eyes and hoped the feeling would stop. It didn't. It got worse. Teri came to my aid, helping me push the IV pole into the bathroom. I closed the door just in time. The diarrhea began again, and with it an intense, shooting pain. Tears poured from my eyes as I let out a scream. I heard a voice call through the door.

"Honey, it's the nurse. May I come in?"

"Okay," I mumbled.

She held a syringe. "This is pain medication," she said gently. "It should give you some relief."

I nodded, so she injected the medicine into my IV line. Then she handed me the Lidocaine. There was no way I could wipe anything across my butt. I asked for an empty cup and she obliged. I reached over and ran the water in the sink until it was warm. After filling the cup, I poured the water down my backside. It stung as it hit the open sores.

I emerged from the bathroom and, with help, made my way back to my chair. The pain was so extreme, that I couldn't sit down. I crawled into the recliner and curled up on my side. I spent more of that session in the bathroom than in my chair. Each time I entered the bathroom, the chemo room filled with sounds of my sobbing. Despite my pep talk and my best intentions, I couldn't imagine continuing for another week.

The next day and all that weekend, I didn't leave bed. My whole body ached. When I wasn't in the bathroom, I slept. It was my only escape from the pain.

On Monday I went to radiation and then came home, climbed back into bed, and drifted off to sleep. Sharp pain woke me and I stumbled out of bed. Doubled over on the toilet, I yelled, "Mark, Mark! Please, Mark!"

He didn't come. Shooting pain radiated from my waist through my abdomen and down my legs. I collapsed onto the floor.

"Michi, what is it?" Teri called from the bedroom.

I was too weak and in too much pain to move. "Get Mark. Please find him."

He came running in. "What's wrong?"

I reached up for him. "I can't do this. I can't take anymore. Please make it stop, make it stop."

He knelt down and kissed my head. "What can I do?"

"Fill the tub and lift me into it. I can't walk."

He did as I requested and carried me to the bath. Looking back, I see that was my breaking point. I had spent a lifetime building emotional walls to prevent feeling this sort of dependency.

I pulled my knees to my chest and put my head down as the tub filled with warm, soothing water. "I'm done, Mark," I cried. "I'm done!"

"What?"

"I'll finish the last chemo but no more radiation. It's destroying my body. I will not go back for another dose. I won't do it."

He was silent for a minute. "But you'll do the chemo."

"Yes, I'll do the last chemo."

"I'll call the radiologist and let him know we're done. You did fine, baby. There were just two sessions left anyway. You don't have to go back. I support you."

I breathed a sigh of relief, knowing that he understood my pain and that he believed I had done the best I could.

Mark holding and supporting me

Aftermath

September to December 2004

I kept my word and finished the last miserable session of chemotherapy, but life didn't magically go back to normal after that. Truth be told, my life would never be the same again. I was changed—physically, mentally, and emotionally. The grief was overwhelming, but I refused to become a prisoner to it. I wasn't sure how to regain my life, so I took it day by day, hoping if I just kept marching forward, it would get better in time.

Even though I was now deemed cancer free, my routine remained unchanged for several weeks. I continued to work, but I spent every free moment in bed—tired, weak, and unable to move. The diarrhea showed no sign of stopping, and although the nausea subsided, the gagging continued.

What if it never stops? What if this is my new reality?

I felt like I had just survived a head-on collision with the universe. My body, totally changed, had become thin and frail. My sunken eyes were rimmed with dark circles. My former porcelain complexion was gone and small, fleshy bumps covered my entire face. I had never experienced bad acne, but now I couldn't escape it. My own image in the mirror repulsed me. I desperately wanted to gain weight, but I had no appetite. Emotionally, I was coming to appreciate my own limitations. I realized I couldn't keep putting everyone else first. I had become all of the things I despised: raw, frail, and needy.

Even though I was technically cured, it turned out I needed more doctors to treat the aftermath of cancer than for the cancer itself. I started with the dermatologist. He read my file and spent two seconds inspecting my face. "Yep, you've been through the ringer. The chemotherapy suppressed your immune system, allowing an infection to form in your skin. The bumps are the visible sign of this infection." He prescribed several medications—an oral antibiotic for six months, a weekly Diflucan pill for the yeast infection that the antibiotic would cause, an antibiotic cream for night and another cream for morning. *Just what I need more medicine and a yeast infection.* I thought.

Then there was sex. I had almost forgotten what it was like. I hadn't experienced it in more than four months and truthfully, I had no desire. I didn't feel sexy or attractive. My body ached. I was in menopause and had only two inches of vaginal canal left. Not only did I lack the desire, the very thought of sex terrified me.

Mark was the perfect husband, gentle, kind, and supportive. He didn't make any advances toward me. He never said a word about his needs. He just focused on me and what I needed to get better. Every night he held me and stroked my head until I fell asleep.

He wasn't getting any play, but I was sure his sex drive hadn't flown the coop with mine. I knew I looked bad, but I was sure he'd gladly have sex with me if I offered it up. I wanted to please him, to share in the emotional intimacy of sex again, but I wasn't sure I could endure the physical pain.

Another month passed. The leaves changed colors, wilted, and fell to the ground. I stayed broken. I thought about the woman I used to be. I longed to feel healthy, sexy, and confident again. I decided it was time to give sex another try, so one night at bedtime, I sat on the edge of the bed naked. Mark climbed in on his side and turned out the light.

"Wanna do it?" I asked.

He turned the light back on and looked at me, puzzled. "Really? You're not joking?"

"We've got to try sooner or later, might as well be now. Right?"

I climbed into bed and slid closer to him. He hesitated. I reached for his hand and gave him the lubricant. He applied it generously and slid his hand between my legs. I pulled back. He followed my lead and retreated.

"Try again," I encouraged him.

His hand against the skin of my thighs and lower abdomen felt weird; some spots ached while others felt like needles piercing my skin. I pulled back again, but then motioned for him to try once more. Tears rolled down my temples and dampened my hair.

Mark pulled back his hand. "Baby, we don't have to do this."

"I'm sorry," was all I could get out. I turned over and cried myself to sleep. I felt so inadequate. I couldn't even enjoy sexual contact with my own husband. How much longer could he take this? How much longer could I?

As the months ticked by, the temperature outside grew colder—much like our bedroom. I went for a follow-up at the radiation center. The doctor asked how sex was going. I admitted it was nonexistent for a number of psychological and physiological reasons. My vagina was dry and hurt all the time. The diarrhea had finally stopped being a daily occurrence, but the pain remained. My bottom was constantly sore and still bled regularly with each bowel movement. My hips were tight and ached all the time. I was experiencing hot flashes and night sweats. Not to mention my self-image was low and the thought of sex made me ill.

He took a deep breath before speaking. "Would you like to talk with a sexual therapist?" I shook my head no. "Radiation causes atrophy: shrinking and dryness. The vagina is a muscle. It will stretch with time and constant use."

I looked at him, puzzled. So was there some special vagina physical therapy?

He reached into a cabinet and pulled out a long, thin box labeled Small. He lifted from the box a hard white plastic object similar to a candle, with a rounded edge.

"This is a dilator," he said. "It will help. Insert it once a day for thirty minutes and apply pressure. Be sure to use a lubricant."

Before I left he handled me a similar box labeled Medium. I assumed I was supposed to work up to the bigger size.

He ordered a CAT scan of my hips to investigate the source of my pain. It didn't show anything unusual, so he referred me to an orthopedic specialist.

At home that evening, I pulled out the dilators and set them on the bathroom counter. *This has to be a joke,* I thought.

I grabbed the tape measure. The small one was six inches long and three and a half inches in diameter. The medium was also six inches long, but four and a half inches around. I didn't know what to think. He might as well have told me to go to the local sex shop and buy a dildo.

I tried to use the small one, but the pain was too great. This seemed so wrong. Dildos were supposed to be the source of great pleasure, not pain. I wasn't ready to put myself through it quite yet.

About a week later I came home and poured myself a glass of wine. I joined Mark in bed and flicked on the TV. I had nearly finished my wine when a warm sensation came over me, and I figured, what the hell. I reached into the drawer of the bedside table and pulled out the dilator and tube of lubricant. Mark kept staring at the TV while watching me out the corner of his eye. I attempted to act like this was normal by cracking a joke.

"Some people eat popcorn while watching TV. I dilate."

I leaned back and took a deep breath. I'd just go for it, like ripping off a Band-Aid. I counted silently to myself—*one, two, three*—and forced the dilator in.

"Shit!"

I took another deep breath and applied a tiny bit of pressure. I could feel the dilator hitting the top wall of my vagina, yet the majority of it was still outside my body. Sharp pain radiated through my vagina and legs. *Thirty minutes! Who is he kidding?* I lasted five minutes before I put it away.

Over the next couple of weeks, I built up my tolerance to twenty minutes at a time. Slowly, the vaginal walls gave. The pain was still ever present, but each time a little more of the dilator fit. Mark and I still weren't having sex, but I could at least see a world where it might be possible. *Baby steps,* I thought.

Thanksgiving arrived. I thought about how grateful I was to be alive. Sure, things weren't perfect. I still hurt a lot. I missed having sex with my husband. I missed my old sense of myself. I hated being in menopause—but I was here. I was still breathing. My thoughts drifted back to Dr. C. She was the one who had discovered the recurrence of my cancer, and we had strongly disagreed regarding treatment and timeline. Now, having survived the cancer, I could see why she had been so insistent on moving fast. I could finally appreciate what she had been trying to do all along: save my life.

I grabbed a pen and note card and scribbled a simple thank you to her. She had never been comfortable with the radical trachelectomy I had had before she became my doctor, so she had always treated me with extra care. I had no doubt that her caution was the reason I was here today.

Another oncologist probably would not have performed the ECC. It wasn't the standard care for follow-up. Her decision to do so had resulted in finding the cancer when the Pap test hadn't. Although the CAT scan had suggested fibroids, Dr. C. had insisted that it was probably a tumor and she had been right.

I was still glad I had decided to go with Dr. D., but I thought Dr. C. should know how grateful I was for her expertise. I dropped off the card at her office the day before Thanksgiving.

After weeks of using the dilator, I felt ready to attempt sex again. I was reluctant, but I knew I had to try. Just as before, I came to bed and blurted out something really romantic, like "Wanna fuck?"

Mark immediately perked up. "Okay. Are you sure?"

"Let's see what happens."

He moved to the middle of the bed and slid his hand toward me. I stopped him. Nothing down there felt particularly good, and some areas were worse than others. Plus, I knew he was in terrible need of personal attention. I reached for the lubricant and applied it to him.

"Oh, your hand feels so good!" he murmured.

When he was really worked up, I applied the lube to myself. It wasn't about my pleasure at this point. I wanted to please him. I knew if sex was ever going to be good for me again, we had to start somewhere.

"Get on top of me," I said. "Just put the tip inside, slowly."

He pressed into me. I gasped and pulled back, trying to avoid the inevitable pain.

I thought about our first time together, the way I had played hard to get, pulling back each time he advanced, until he finally refused to continue, telling me he wasn't going to force me to have sex with him. I had been disappointed, wanting him to be aggressive and forceful, but even then he had been gentle. I tried to hold on to that image. I wanted to remember how good the sex had been that evening.

"Are you okay?" He started to move away.

I grabbed his butt and stopped him from pulling out. "Just get it over with quickly. It's all about you." I turned my face away from him.

"I don't want to hurt you."

"Please, just do it." *How romantic,* I thought. *I'm sure he's turned on now!* I pulled a pillow over my face and bit into it so as not to scream. The pain was incredible. His penis felt like a knife slicing through me. I cried into the pillow, silently praying it would end quickly.

Less than five minutes later, he was finished. "Are you okay? Did I hurt you too much?" he asked, visibly concerned

"I'm fine. Please run the tub," I mumbled through the tears.

He kissed my forehead. "Thank you," he said, and then hopped out of bed and turned on the bath.

The sex had been awful for me, as I had expected, but I was curious how it had felt to him. I wanted him to tell me it was great, that I had met his needs. Maybe that would make me feel whole again. The next morning without any warning, I hit him with, "So how was it?"

He looked like a deer caught in the headlights. I'm sure it was a question he was hoping I would never ask.

"Come on. Was it good? Did it feel different?"

"Umm … yes. Just much tighter."

Not such a bad thing. "And …? Tell me more."

"I could feel the end of it. I think. It was shallow. The main difference was just that it hurt you. It was hard to enjoy myself when I knew I was causing you pain. I don't like hurting you or seeing you suffer."

I kissed him and then wrapped my arms around him. "It just has to be this way for now. In time, the doctors say, it will feel good again. You have to believe. In the meantime, we just have to do it." As he nodded, I wondered who I thought I was kidding. Even I didn't believe that.

I followed up with the orthopedist about my hips. He reviewed the CAT scan but didn't see a clear explanation for my pain. I told him about my cancer and the pelvic radiation. He explained that in rare circumstances, radiation could cause necrosis of the hips, also called dead bone disease, but he emphasized that it was rare. He suspected the radiation had not only caused atrophy in the vaginal muscles, but also in the muscles of the hips. He arranged for me to see a physical therapist three times a week, and gave me daily exercises to do at home for strengthen and lengthen the affected muscles of my hip and pelvic region.

Christmas 2004: Mark, Charlee, George and me with my new perm

Now that we had dealt with all of the things causing me pain, it was time to deal with the other fallout from my ordeal. Something had to be done about my appearance. I hated the way I looked. I was too tall to be so thin. I missed my ass and my boobs, which had all but disappeared during treatment. I had gained five pounds since treatment ended and now weighed 117 pounds. It was a start, but I was still too skinny. I started adding weight-gaining shakes to my morning routine. It was hard, but I forced myself to eat, and every night I did the exercises my therapist gave me.

My hair was a disaster, limp and dull. It hadn't fallen out, but it might as well have. I went to the hairstylist, desperate for help. She suggested a perm for added body. I had never had one and it sounded scary, but I figured she was the professional, not me.

She used large rollers, and in no time flat, she transformed my look. My hair was different: fuller, bigger, a bit like a rocker chick from the eighties. I wasn't thrilled, but at least it was an improvement.

The year was almost over, with Christmas just a week away. Three months had passed since the end of my treatment, and it was time for my follow-up with Dr. D. He gave me a big hug when he entered the examining room. I really appreciated his personal touch. He made me feel like a long-lost friend, not just another cancer case. Then, as usual, a medical student updated him on my case. I gave him more details, including the painful sex, rectal bleeding, and incontinence. I had been told the latter would stop after radiation, but here I was three months later, still shitting my pants at least once a week. To say it was embarrassing would be an understatement.

He performed a pelvic exam and confirmed that my rectum was still torn. He referred me to another specialist for my bowel issues. Then he did a Pap test. I had no cervix left, so he scraped the top portion of the vaginal canal. The Pap had missed my cancer both times before, so I wasn't very confident in it now, but protocol required it.

He asked many questions about our sex life, but I didn't have much to tell. He encouraged me to have patience, reminding me that any muscle shrinks without regular use, so I should keep having sex. He assured me it would get better.

I knew he was probably right, but honestly, I just couldn't imagine the day when sex would actually feel good. I was worried that my love life would never be normal again.

New Beginnings ──────────────────

Winter to summer 2005

January 2005 brought with it the hope of a new beginning. My thirtieth birthday was less than three weeks away. I couldn't wait. Maybe most people don't share my enthusiasm and joy when turning thirty, but I was eager to start a new decade of my life with a clean slate. I had spent the early part of my twenties searching for myself, and the last half battling cancer. I was glad to bid my twenties farewell, to start fresh and cancer free.

Wanting both to have fun and spend quality time with my girlfriends and my grandmother, I planned a trip home to D.C. When Caryn volunteered to throw a little celebration for me, I gladly accepted.

I sent her the list of people I wanted there, and she did the rest. The next week, I received my invitation in the mail:

> As we enter a new decade with Michi, please join us
> in celebrating her thirtieth birthday, recent marriage,
> triumphant survival and a new beginning.
> Cocktails and Appetizers
> Saturday, January 15, 2005, at 8 p.m.

I smiled as I turned her words over in my head. She was right. The battle had been difficult, but now was truly the time to embrace life and start again. I arrived in D.C. a week before the party and stayed with Caryn.

My number one priority was spending time with my aging grandmother. She was unable to travel now, and during my illness I had missed her so much. Each day I rose early and drove to her house. Grandma and I spent hours together laughing, talking, and eating. As we reminisced, I was overwhelmed with emotion. She had always made me feel safe, protected, and strong; and she had inspired me and made me believe I could accomplish anything I set my mind to. That attitude had helped carry me through the cancer battle. In that sense, even though she hadn't been able to be with me in person, she helped save my life.

I still wasn't feeling particularly strong or empowered. In fact, I was barely keeping my head above water, surviving from one minute to the next. Spending time with her reminded me of all the lessons she had taught me, most importantly to keep going.

"Life is a journey and cancer is not your destiny. It was just a stop along the way," she said as she smiled at me.

She told me I would rebuild myself and turn this terrible experience into something positive. I looked into her eyes and believed. In that moment, I chose not to cry anymore over what I had lost to cancer. Instead I would focus on what I had gained: the rest of my life. I would laugh more and cry less, embrace my future and the rest of the amazing journey that still lay ahead.

The day of the party, I went with Caryn to pick up the cake. It was a yellow cake with white icing and colored balloons. It read Happy 30th Birthday, congratulations on your wedding.

"What, nothing about the cancer?" I asked.

"No, what would I put?"

"And kicking the cancer's butt again!"

Caryn giggled. "Let's add it."

The salesclerk did as we instructed, while looking at us like we had lost our minds.

Back at home, Caryn prepared all the food while I watched. Cooking was not my specialty, but at least I could stand the smell and taste of food again.

The guests started arriving, and we ate, drank, and laughed late into the night. I shared openly with my friends about my experience, and for the first time I was able to joke about it. I didn't feel sorry for myself anymore. Instead, I felt strong again and proud of my journey. It was the best birthday party I ever had. I was totally happy, with one exception. I couldn't stop thinking about babies. I had had these "baby visions" after my first bout with cancer, but this time it was different. Babies crept into my head at the weirdest times, like during work meetings, in traffic, and even on date night with Mark. I noticed every baby and pregnant woman within a hundred yards of me. I wondered if I really wanted children, or if I was merely grieving the loss of my ability to have them.

I was never really enthusiastic about kids before the cancer. In fact, they scared me. It wasn't just that I was worried I might have them and then change my mind; it was that they seemed so alien to me. I didn't speak their language or have a clue what to do with them. Now being a mom was all I could think about. Pregnant women seemed to stalk me. They had never registered on my radar before, but now they seemed to be everywhere. I found myself watching them and envying them.

What would it feel like to have a child growing inside of me?

I imagined myself with a huge belly trying to work or do dishes (my least favorite chore). Tears filled my eyes every time. My embryos were frozen, but without a uterus, I would never be able to carry them myself. I mourned something I would never experience.

February came and the many doctor appointments continued. Only this time I embraced them. My outlook had totally changed after the visit with my grandmother. Cancer was just an inconvenience, a bump in the road on my journey. I no longer let my physical pain control my mood, day, or life. I was just glad to be alive.

The issues with my bowels improved slightly, but I still needed help. I followed up with the gastroenterologist, as Dr. D. had instructed. After an unpleasant colonoscopy, I learned I was suffering from radiation colitis in addition to the tear in my rectum. The tear was causing the bleeding, while the colitis was the culprit behind the loose and sometimes uncontrollable stools.

He prescribed suppositories and more creams. It seemed like I now owned a cream for every medical ailment imaginable. The gastroenterologist suggested I give my body more time to heal before we proceeded with any more aggressive treatments. I agreed. I wasn't going to volunteer for more treatments. I needed a vacation.

He told me that if there wasn't progress, the next step would be to inject Botox into the tissue around the tear, paralyzing it and allowing the area to heal. *Botox? The wrinkle stuff?* He explained that the procedure would be done in the surgery center, so my insurance company wouldn't consider it cosmetic surgery and would cover the cost. It would be a facelift for my butt! Just the thought made me laugh.

The following week I left for a meeting in Atlanta, my first week-long business trip since my illness. On Monday morning, I boarded the plane in my black power suit and heels, feeling every inch the formidable businesswoman. The lady at the counter upgraded me to first class since I had so many frequent flyer points. *Lucky me!* I thought. *This is going to be a good trip.* I tucked away my belongings and made myself cozy in seat 2D, a window seat. An older, distinguished man in a dark single-breasted suit sat down next to me. I dozed off during takeoff. When I woke up, he was reading the newspaper. I reached into my briefcase and pulled out my laptop, only to find the battery was dead. He noticed me quickly open and then shut the computer.

"I hate when that happens to me," he said.

"Me too."

We continued to chat during the flight. As we neared Atlanta, the flight attendant made the announcement for all passengers to restore their seats and tray tables to the upright position and buckle up. Just then I felt my stomach turn and pressure in my bowels. *Oh no. Oh no. Oh please. Not now. Not here.*

I squeezed my butt cheeks together. Meanwhile, the gentleman next to me continued talking.

"So do you like living in Tennessee?" he asked, oblivious to my impending catastrophe.

"Um … yeah. It's great." I smiled and squeezed tighter, but it was no use. There was nothing I could do to stop it. The smell hit my nostrils and burned. I couldn't believe it. *I had just shit my pants in first class!*

The businessman simply smiled at me and continued talking as if he didn't notice a thing. The plane was landing, so I couldn't get up and go to the restroom—well, unless I wanted to get arrested. Moving about during takeoff and landing was not only frowned upon, but potentially criminal after 9/11. There was nothing else to do now but sit and wait. It took everything in me not to laugh hysterically. What thirty-year-old woman shits her pants in first class?

The plane landed, and I tied my suit jacket around my waist. I grabbed my bags and raced for the bathroom. I was meeting colleagues in the airport, so I needed to act fast. Ducking into a stall, I dropped my pants. The smell almost knocked me out. Again, I invoked my grandmother's wisdom. *This is just a bump in the road. A smelly, embarrassing bump, but a really funny bump.* Luckily, I still kept extra panties and wipes in my briefcase in case of an emergency. I changed and dumped the used underwear into the wastebasket.

This was too ridiculous and too funny not to share, so I called Caryn. "I shit my …" I was laughing so hard I could barely get the words out. "My pants in first class."

"You what?"

"Shit my pants."

"In first class on the plane?"

"You got it."

She began to laugh uncontrollably. She said, "I'm so sorry," followed by more laughter. I was grateful that I—and my close friend—found some humor in what was an otherwise mortifying situation.

I approached my sex life much like my experience in first class. It sucked, but feeling bad wasn't going to change it and laughing about it was so much more fun. I jokingly started calling myself "the born again virgin." I did have a new vagina, after all, custom made to fit my husband. Well, after some dilating. Now, how many women could say that?

Mark and I followed the doctor's advice and practiced having sex once a week. Of course, this was almost always after a glass of wine, which helped ease the vulnerability I felt about my body image and performance ability. It was increasingly hard to relax my mind and enjoy any physical contact. Mark attempted to stimulate me using foreplay, but I wasn't into it and usually stopped him. It not only hurt, it made me feel uncomfortable and inadequate. Sex was now a task rather than an enjoyable experience. I just wanted to do it and be done. I was rigid, tense, and flinched at the touch of his hands on my skin. My actions subconsciously established boundaries and created distance between us.

Mark had always been a thoughtful lover with significant endurance, but my newly imposed limits forced him to change tactics. These days he was lucky to get five minutes of action. He made the best of the situation and tried to follow my lead. He was careful and gentle; he wanted me to enjoy myself as much as possible.

The truth was that as much I wanted to enjoy it, I hated every second of it. He felt like sandpaper sliding in and out of me. I fought back the tears as much as I could and hid my face beneath a pillow. I wanted to please him, but having sex was torturous. I cried almost every time, and often retreated to a hot bath immediately after we finished. I couldn't even remember what it felt like to climax. I was a stranger in my own body.

Winter gave way to spring, which slowly became summer. As the time passed, I learned a few tricks. After a few days or weeks of no sex, the first time always hurt the worst. But I discovered that if we did it two nights in a row, the second night was always better. Sex for me now was like breaking in a new pair of shoes. They hurt like hell the first few times you wore them, but after a while, you could wear them for several hours without killing your feet. It was the same way with my post-cancer genitalia. The more often we had sex, the more flexible my vaginal muscles became, which meant we could have sex for longer periods of time before the pain became too much. But two nights in a row was definitely my limit. After that I usually needed at least a week to recover. At this rate, I feared I'd never again enjoy sex or experience the joy of an orgasm.

Before I knew it, a year had come and gone since I had beat cancer. I stood in front of the mirror, staring at myself. I still didn't recognize the image looking back at me, despite the help of the dermatologist and the '80s-style perm. My hair remained limp and lifeless. The new growth didn't absorb the chemicals from the hair dye or perm in quite the same manner as the hair that had gone through chemo. Layers of different shades and textures formed around my head like rings in a tree—markers of where I had been.

On a whim, I jumped in the car and drove to the hair salon. Lucky for me, the shop wasn't busy and my favorite hairdresser was available. I plopped in her chair. "Cut it off!"

"What, a few inches?"

"No, all of it. Get the buzzer and take it off. I want a new start!"

Stunned, she stared at me like I had lost my mind. Eventually, she picked up the scissors and began cutting, cautiously shaping it into a perfect bob.

"Shorter!" I demanded.

"Let's do this slowly. I can always cut more, but I can't add any."

"However you want to do it, just go shorter."

She turned the chair away from the mirror, limiting my vision and preventing me from commenting as she cut. Each time she thought she was done, she spun me back to the mirror. I took a quick glance and said, "Shorter!" After three times, she finally got the point. The next time I saw myself in the mirror, I looked like a different person. The result was a perfect pixie cut, short, sassy, and—dare I say it—even sexy. She looked at me, scared, waiting for my reaction.

"I love it!" It was just what I needed. A new version of me, a new beginning.

Reclaiming My Sexuality

Fall 2005 to spring 2006

My new look revitalized my confidence and I started to feel sexy again, but actually enjoying sex remained another story. I still hated to have Mark explore my body. I never knew what might feel okay and what might hurt like hell, so I couldn't relax and enjoy being with him. I wanted to turn off my thoughts and simply be in the moment, but I couldn't. My body had been through hell and was forever changed by it. The positions, caresses, and experiences I had once found pleasurable felt different now. I had to relearn my body, but I was determined to find new ways to enjoy intimacy.

I left no rock unturned in my search. I read sexual books and magazines. I talked to my friends about their love lives, hoping I might learn a new trick. I even explored my own body in an attempt to discover the ways Mark should touch me to stimulate my desire. I experimented with a variety of vibrators in search of the lost orgasm. There was no immediate payoff for my diligence, but I kept at it. I hoped if I continued putting one foot in front of the other, eventually I'd reach that point of enjoyment again.

I was still experiencing menopausal night sweats, waking up nearly every night freezing and drenched, but the daytime symptoms lessened with time. Then, about a year and a half after the treatment ended, something changed. The night sweats faded away, and instead some nights I had vivid sexual dreams. I woke up very turned on. I had never experienced dreams like these before. I shared them with Mark, in all their graphic detail, which led to a new level of intimacy between us. Before long I was not only thinking about sex, but I actually wanted it again. *Hallelujah!*

Even with the increased desire, I still experienced pain during sexual contact. The pain was less intense than the previous year, but still present. A few months after I started sharing my dreams with Mark, I found myself actually aroused before bed. I wanted Mark's lips against mine. My breasts tingled, and I longed to feel him caress my body—my breasts, back, stomach, and ass. But I didn't want his hand anywhere near my crotch. Mark knew by now where he could and couldn't touch, so I could relax without feeling the need to control the situation. I let go and cleared my mind of the thoughts and fears that had haunted me since the cancer. After ten minutes of foreplay, I climbed on top of him and carefully lowered myself. The movement was slow and deep. Within minutes, I found myself in the midst of the long lost orgasm. I was elated. *Oh my God, oh my God, yes! Finally, it happened. I can climax!*

Even after that orgasm, sex was still difficult and painful most of the time. But every now and then, all the elements lined up perfectly—physically, emotionally, and physiologically—and the sex was mind-blowing. Once upon a time, having an orgasm was a given for me, but now it was like finding a needle in a haystack. Still, each time it happened, I learned a little more about what worked. Just knowing it was possible gave me hope. And once we discovered that it was possible, we kept looking for more. Be sure to check my tips on page 174.

Two-Year Checkup, Round Two

August 2006

On August 15, I awoke with a feeling of déjà vu. It was time for my usual three-month checkup with Dr. D., but this wasn't just any appointment. It was an anniversary. Two years had passed since I had finished my chemo and radiation. Nearly two and a half years had gone by since I'd learned that my cancer had returned. It seemed so unreal.

After my first bout with cancer, I hadn't been too worried about the two-year checkup. In fact, I had been excited, thinking I was so over the cancer. Then, with a simple phone call a few days later, everything had changed and my world was turned upside down.

Today has to be different. The cancer has to be gone for good.

Mark and I showered and dressed, prepping for the day ahead of us. As we arrived at the doctor's office, I sprang out of the car before Mark had a chance to put it in park.

"Whoa, girl!" he called as I strode toward the door. "Not so fast!"

I hadn't even realized I was leaving him behind. I was so ready to march in there and get this checkup over with.

We proceeded upstairs into the waiting room, which, at 8:53 in the morning, was already full. After a few minutes, the receptionist called my name. I paid the co-pay, and she handed me a laptop so I could update my condition and information for the doctor.

Just as I completed the form, the nurse, a pretty girl with short black hair, called my name. I followed her back to a computer outside the exam rooms.

"Have a seat," she said. "I just want to get your vitals. We don't have a room open yet." She took my blood pressure and measured my height. She looked up at me and asked, "So, how are you doing?"

I laughed. "Well, I have a few complaints, but overall pretty good, I'd say. At this point it's all relative. When you've been to hell and back, today's complaints aren't that bad."

She chuckled. "I guess you're right."

"Michelle!" someone yelled. I looked up to see my chemo nurse. "I was just thinking about you. I remember that day at chemo when you were so sick and screaming in the bathroom." My chemo nurse turned to the nurse with short black hair. "The radiation just burned her up. It was so terrible." No one said anything for a long moment, and then she changed the subject. "Where's that handsome husband of yours?"

I told her he was in the waiting room. She gave me a hug and quickly disappeared.

"You can go back to the waiting room," the dark-haired nurse said, "and I'll call you again when a room opens."

At 9:45 she finally called me back to an exam room. She took my weight and announced that it was 121 pounds. *Well, that's progress,* I thought. I had started treatment at a healthy 130 pounds. My weight dropped to 109 pounds at the lowest point of chemo and radiation, a symbol of all the abuse my body had taken. My weight was still low, but it was a sign that I was healing, that things were looking up, that I was getting back to my old self.

Ten minutes later the door opened and in walked a young Middle Eastern woman in a white coat. "Hello, Mich—" she started, but I interrupted her introduction.

"You're the medical student here to gather information for Dr. D."

"Correct. I suppose you've been here a few times."

"Just a few."

I gave her a quick overview of my case and filled her in on my ongoing issues from the radiation treatment. She left the room to brief the doctor. While she was gone, I reflected back on previous visits and how I used to eavesdrop at the door every time a student left to update the doctor, afraid they were telling each other things they wouldn't say to me. Over the years, I realized my doctor was just training the medical students, not trying to keep things from me. Eventually, I stopped trying to listen and just sat patiently. My inner control freak had gone twelve rounds with cancer and had learned a valuable lesson: sometimes you just have to let go and trust the process.

Dr. D. entered the room a few minutes later, followed by his student. "Hello, how are you?" he said, greeting me with an embrace. No matter how many times I saw Dr. D., I never got tired of that friendly and personable greeting. He had an amazing way of making me feel like I was visiting an old friend instead of a doctor. When you have spent as much time at the doctor's as I have, that's no small thing.

We reviewed the list of complaints from my last visit: blood in the stool, urinary incontinence, vaginal dryness. You know, the usual. Nothing had changed since my last visit, and he recommended that I continue seeing my other doctors for these issues.

"I hear you have had an increase in yeast infections recently," he added.

"Yes, about one per month. This concerns me, because each time prior to the cancer being identified, I experienced frequent yeast infections. But I'm sure you'll say they weren't related."

"No, they weren't directly connected, but these infections do tell us something about how well your immune system is or isn't working. When you have cancer, your immune system is weakened, so it's possible there's a connection. You know your body. Let's take a look and then talk some more."

He slipped out the door, allowing me to change. I undressed from the waist down and positioned myself on the table with the little white sheet draped over me. Minutes later, he returned with his student. She sat on the circular stool between my feet as Dr. D. handed her something.

"Are you going to do my exam?" I asked her.

"Is that all right with you?" she asked, looking up at me.

Dr. D. replied, "We're going to do it together."

"Sure, go ahead," I said. "If you're going to learn, I guess you have to do it."

He talked her through the wet-prep Pap test and my exam. While he instructed her, I joked that I should be a professor by now, since I'd been helping him teach his students over the years. He agreed but said I was too young to be a full professor; he would name me a junior professor.

They switched places so he could examine me himself. "Looks good, but if you're concerned, we will run another CAT scan," he said. I sat quietly for a moment. We had just done one three months earlier, and it had come back clear. The yeast infections did concern me, though. I wanted to be smart by listening to my body, but at the same time, I didn't want to give in to every little fear.

"Let's see how the next few months go," I finally said. "If anything changes, I'll call. Maybe the yeast infection is just something my body is more susceptible to than others and nothing more. I do feel well otherwise, and my energy level is good."

With that, we agreed to see each other again in three months.

Before I left, Dr. D. asked me if I'd heard the great news. The Federal Drug Administration had approved the new vaccine for HPV.

"Just think about how many women it will help," he said. "I believe this vaccine will help eradicate cervical cancer in our lifetime. Now we just need young women to start getting vaccinated." He paused before continuing, "It's optional and there is some stigma to overcome."

The vaccine had made headlines lately, mostly for the controversy it had stirred up. The media touted the drug as a way to prevent HPV instead of a way to protect girls against cervical cancer. For many people, HPV still had a stigma as a STD, and was considered synonymous with promiscuity.

Many parents didn't want to believe their daughters needed it, while others thought they had time to decide later. They were missing the fact that the vaccine worked best if it was administered before a woman's first sexual experience. I knew HPV could happen to anyone—even after just one sexual encounter—and I also knew firsthand the brutal realities of cervical cancer. The media reported that many parents were resisting the vaccine because they felt it somehow gave their daughters permission to have sex. I didn't agree. If there was something that could prevent cervical cancer, getting it seemed like a no-brainer. After all, none of us get into a car thinking we were going to have an accident, but we still buy insurance and buckled our kids into car seats. As much as most parents might not want to admit it, teens are curious about sex. Sooner or later they all try it, and I didn't know anyone who had ever called home for permission first. *If you could protect your daughter against a disease that could cause cancer, why wouldn't you?*

"I'll tell everyone I know about it," I said. "If there's a way to prevent other women from going through this, I want to help."

Dr. D gave me a hug and left the room. I grabbed my things and walked outside into the bright sunshine, confident that my cancer was gone for good.

Finding My Voice

Late 2006 to early 2007

Something was nagging at me. I wasn't sure what it was, but it was getting stronger every day. I was successful in my career, happily married, and surrounded by friends, but still I felt something was missing. Through the years, I had attempted to fill this emotional hole by exceeding in all the ways I believed were expected of me. I set goals and checked them off. Like a Girl Scout collecting merit badges, I was always in search of the next accomplishment. Each success brought a sense of pride but ultimately left me feeling unfulfilled. I mastered the challenges life put in front of me, but I didn't know what I really wanted.

I felt like my career had chosen me, instead of me choosing it. I had taken a job when I was seventeen and before I knew it, my after-school job had turned into my career. Over the years, it seemed like every time I thought about changing careers, I got a promotion with additional benefits and challenges. My career provided the financial security I had never had growing up, and for that I was grateful, but I knew it wasn't my life's calling. When I met Mark, I was searching: searching for my future, searching for my calling, searching for my true self.

Mark was so different than I was. He did exactly what he wanted, when he wanted. He took risks and tried new things. He listened to his inner voice and desires, and made choices that aligned with them. He did not allow fear to hold him back; he confronted it head-on. He relished his accomplishments and enjoyed each moment. I both appreciated and envied these characteristics. I wanted desperately to be more carefree and to chase my dreams, but I didn't know what those dreams were.

Mark's goal was to work for himself. He had talked about it since the day I met him. When he finally had the opportunity to start a company during my illness, I pleaded with him not to do it. I wanted him to wait until life was more stable. I feared the uncertainty and financial burden it might bring. But he did not let fear—his or mine—stop him. He stayed true to his vision and succeeded in building a business. I longed to feel that sense of purpose.

I thought about my career and all its different facets and responsibilities. The aspects I enjoyed the most were working with others, public speaking, and training and providing professional development. Then I analyzed my interests outside of my job. There was cervical cancer again, staring me in the face. I couldn't just stuff it away and go back to my life. It had become such a part of my story and my identity. It had forever altered my view of the world, and for the better. Cancer was no longer this horrible event in my life, but instead, somehow a gift. It gave me a new voice and I wanted to use that voice to speak out.

I talked to anyone who would listen. The funny thing was, most people were eager to listen. Nearly every woman I talked to had questions and stories about her own experiences that she was yearning to communicate. "You're so easy to talk to," I heard over and over again. I became the friend with whom everyone shared their "girly" stories. The strange part was that the more I talked to other women, the better I felt. All that sharing had a tremendous healing power.

One afternoon it finally came together for me while I was lifting weights. As I powered through my back and biceps workout, my mind wandered. How could I leverage my skills and the parts of my career I most enjoyed with my passion for cervical cancer awareness? Then it hit me like a ton of bricks: I had found my calling as an advocate for women's health.

I wrote an article for a women's cancer magazine about my experience. A few months later I went to a meeting of other young survivors. Talking with them made me understand I wasn't alone. By telling my own story, I might be able to bring that kind of comfort to other women who were just beginning the long road I had walked. Or better yet, maybe I could help educate women about preventing the disease in the first place, as well educating them about fertility preservation and the need for women to be their own health care advocates.

Today, I want to empower other women to take a proactive approach to their health and health care. I firmly believe I wouldn't be here if I hadn't listened to my body, and if I hadn't had the courage to act on that wisdom. I know for certain I wouldn't have had the choice to be a mother. Our society does not support women talking about sex, sexuality, and their bodies; and the structure of the medical establishment doesn't encourage patients to ask questions or push back. I want to change that. When a young woman tells me that after hearing my story, she got her first Pap test in five years or asked for an HPV test, I feel good. It's as if everything I went through happened for a reason. If I can help protect even one woman, then my own journey—land mines and all—was worth it. My advocacy started as way to help other young women, but it has given me so much more.

Me presenting at a physician education dinner given by TN Cancer
Coalition and Nurse Practitioners in Women's Health (NPWH)

Prayers

Spring 2007

Nearly three years after I beat cancer for the second time, I was driving north on Mississippi Highway 61 as the sun set over the endless cotton fields. I was antsy and couldn't wait to get home. I loved my job, but being a district manager for a retail chain meant lots of time on the road. I was tired from a long workweek and eager to see Mark and sleep in my own bed. My drive was boring; miles of flat land interrupted only by an occasional patch of trees. There were never any decent radio stations, so on this stretch of road, I often did a lot of thinking.

As I stared ahead, the sun dipped toward the horizon and the sky filled with bright shades of pinks and purples and oranges. *I'm so grateful for another day and another sunset. Thank you, God! Thank you for this moment.* My mind wandered back to other sunsets in my life, all the ones I had taken for granted. The simple things in life I was too busy to appreciate before I realized how quickly they could disappear.

As I drove along, I thought about Mark, my wonderful, loving husband and friend. Smiling, I recalled images of him in the early days—my carefree beach boy riding his skateboard, anti-responsibility and with no thoughts of ever tying the knot. Oh, how things had changed. Not only had he tied the knot, he had seen a sick wife to the edge of death and nursed her back to health.

My mind wandered to thoughts of our favorite time together: naked cuddle time. I had been so worried that our sexual problems would drive Mark away, but instead we discovered a secret intimacy in those days, months, and years after my treatment; a closeness we might not have known otherwise. I always knew our love was special, but my cancer proved the real depth of our bond. My eyes filled with tears—tears of gratitude for all that cancer had taught me, and tears of joy for our wonderful life and dreams for the future.

Once upon a time many years ago, I was too busy and too scared to consider having children. Now the idea weighed on my mind constantly. I yearned to hold a little one, to look into his or her face and see Mark's freckles and my eyes looking back at me—a living testament to our love. Was I supposed to be a mother? I didn't know at this point. And yet I had undergone a fertility-saving procedure in order to preserve my ability to choose. Then, when my cancer returned, I managed to freeze my embryos, my little miracle Maybe Babies. That had almost cost me my life. Why, when confronted with so many obstacles, had I fought so hard for the opportunity to be a mother some day?

Mark didn't feel the same push toward parenthood. He couldn't picture himself as a father and didn't see how children would fit into our life. He considered them too much responsibility. Given his reluctance, I hadn't explored my options for becoming a mother in any depth. Yet. The bit of research I had conducted on surrogacy was too overwhelming to digest.

The prices ranged from about $50,000 to $150,000 for the total process, which included hiring an agency to locate someone to carry the baby and paying that person, and the legal fees and medical costs. And I had thought the first fertility treatments were expensive! I had no idea how the average middle-class couple could ever afford it.

It was dark as I neared Tunica, Mississippi. Only an hour left to go. I checked the radio, knowing it was futile. Yep, still no good stations.

I decided to use my last hour to talk to the one person who I knew could help me make sense of all the questions swirling in my head. I didn't know what the future held for me, but someone else did.

Hello, God. It's me. Thank you for today. Thank you for saving my life not once, but twice. I don't know why you saved me, but I'm sure glad you did! Thank you for filling my life with so much love—the love of my husband, family, and friends.

God, I'm so confused. Are Mark and I meant to be parents, parents of our own biological children? I really want to be a mother. Mark isn't so sure. God, please continue to guide us and to help us understand your will. If we are supposed to be parents, help Mark realize it. If we aren't, please help me to accept your choice. Oh, you should know I've already picked out names!

Thank you, God! In Jesus Christ's name I ask my prayers. Amen.

I pulled in my driveway just after 10:00 p.m. Carrying my briefcase and luggage, I reached for the knob to the back door. The door opened before I touched it. Mark was standing on the other side waiting for me. I dropped the bags and threw myself into his embrace. *Home, sweet home.*

"Welcome home, baby!" he said as he squeezed me tightly.

I took in a deep breath. *This is what it all was for.*

I lost a lot to cancer, but along the way I found so much more: the love of my life, the courage to speak up and speak out, and a sense of peace about the future. *This is my life, and it is beautiful.*

Epilogue

Parenthood was a touchy subject between Mark and me for the next few years. I could absolutely picture myself as a mother and could clearly see our life with children. Mark was another story. He worried that it would radically change our way of life for the worse. I thought I could convince him and found ways to work it into almost every conversation we had. This behavior frustrated Mark, to say the least. I kept challenging him to consider the possibility and he kept insisting he had no interest.

I'm not sure how or why, but things started to change one spring day in 2007. Mark was on a golfing trip with a bunch of friends. He called home and said, "I can't wait to see you and I have a surprise."

"You want to have a baby, don't you?" I blurted out.

"How did you know that's what I was going to say? Wow. Anyway, so I was throwing a football in the yard with the guys today and thought about my days of playing ball. Some of the guys were talking about their kids and in that moment I could picture myself as a father."

It was almost as if someone had flipped a switch in him. I was elated.

"Yay! I'm so excited. Now we—"

Mark interrupted me. "Slow down. I didn't mean I want a baby today, I'm just saying I could see it in the future. We'll talk about it when I get home."

I was just happy to be able to have the conversation.

Over the next several months, we discussed what our life would look like with a baby, how we would parent, and how we felt about raising children. Finally, almost a year after that weekend with his friends, Mark decided he was ready. The next step was finding a surrogate to carry our child. (The term "gestational host" is actually more accurate, but for the sake of ease, I will refer to the general idea of someone else carrying our child as surrogacy).

Our journey through surrogacy could be another book in itself. Our first surrogate miscarried in October of 2008 at just eight weeks pregnant. It was a hard blow after such a long journey, but we had come so far and I wasn't about to give up. A month later, I started my search for a second surrogate and found her. On February 27, 2009, our last two embryos were implanted. The next ten days were tense until we got a glimmer of hope with a positive pregnancy test. At eight weeks, an ultrasound confirmed our baby had a heartbeat and was growing well. I was overcome with joy. I spent the next nine months experiencing pregnancy much the way a man does. I knew my baby was growing inside our surrogate, but it was surreal. I worried whether I would be able to bond with my baby. I had no idea what to expect, and my anxiety about motherhood still haunted me. At the same time, I daydreamed about having a little girl and doing all the mother-daughter things I wish my mom had done with me.

On October 27, 2009, Riley Grier Whitlock was born three weeks early at seven pounds thirteen ounces. I can't put into words how amazing it was to see her being born, but any fears I had about bonding went right out the window the moment I laid eyes on her. I knew instantly that I would do everything in my power to protect her, like a lioness does her cub.

Within a few days of her birth, our bond was cemented. I knew the sound of her cries, and my touch comforted her. Every time I sat holding her, looking down at her little hand gripping my finger, I fell in love with her all over again.

Cancer had made me face my greatest fear: motherhood. Considering all the pieces that had to fall into place in order for Riley Grier to be here, I'm amazed. I had to confront my complex relationship with my mother and all the anxiety it created in me. Initially, I gave in to the fears by telling myself I didn't want to be a mother. When I was first diagnosed, I fought to keep my fertility mostly out of stubbornness and a desire to control my life and my future. I was more concerned with preserving my choice than with having a child. But as I battled for my life and my fertility, something changed in me. Cancer taught me how precious life really is. It forced me to outgrow the hard shell I had created around myself after my mother left. I learned that I was not my mother and that my choices would be different than hers.

Riley Grier fills places in my heart I never even knew were there. She's the light of my life. I love watching her grow and explore, and I revel in seeing the world through her eyes. Loving her is the easiest and most natural thing I've ever done. My eyes fill with tears as I think about what a miracle she is and just how grateful I am for the opportunity to be her mom. I will never understand why my mother didn't choose to raise me, but it doesn't matter today. I know I will never choose to be separate from my sweet baby girl.

Mark also took immediately to parenthood. He is a natural with our baby girl and the type of daddy or papí, as he likes to be called, every woman wants for her child. As I watch Mark and Riley Grier together, I know dreams do come true and they are the answer to mine.

Mommy and Riley Grier—my angel

HPV and Cervical Cancer Facts —————————

According to the American Cancer Society and Center for Disease Control

Statistics 2012:
- Cervical cancer is the fourth most common cancer in woman worldwide, with approximately 528,000 new cases each year and nearly 266,00 deaths.
- In the US, 12,900 new patients develop invasive cervical cancer each year and 4,100 die.
- *Almost all* sexually active adults will have an HPV infection before the age of fifty.
- A woman dies approximately every two minutes from cervical cancer.
- Millions of women have abnormal Pap Test annually. Most do not develop cervical cancer.
- There are over seventy-nine million people living with HPV today in the United States. Another 14 million are diagnosed annually.
- Approximately 26,800 cases of cancer are attributed to an HPV infection including but not limited to: cervical, vaginal, vulvar, anal, penile, throat and mouth.

HPV Facts:
- HPV is easily transmitted.
- HPV is transmitted through genital contact, skin-to-skin.
- HPV is so common, it is considered the "common cold" of sexually transmitted infections.
- Although almost all women will have contracted the HPV virus by the time they are fifty, for most of them their immune systems will clear it without any signs or symptoms.
- HPV is now linked to several cancers, including but not limited to: cervical, vaginal, vulva, throat, mouth, lung, and anal cancer.
- The average HPV-positive person has had 2.1 sexual partners.

- Anyone can contract it, regardless of ethnicity or socioeconomic background.
- Limiting the number of sexual partners and using condoms helps reduce the risk of contracting HPV. However, condoms do not provide 100 percent protection against HPV.
- Having HPV is not a sign of infidelity or promiscuity. It only takes one sexual act, with or without a condom, to contract the virus. HPV can lie dormant for years, so there is little way to know when or from whom one got the virus.

Cervical Cancer Risk Factors:

- HPV, specifically HPV 16 and 18. These two strains alone account for 70 percent of all cervical cancers. However, HPV is present in 99 percent of all cervical cancers.
- Multiple sexual partners, although it only takes one partner with or without a condom to contract HPV.
- Early sexual activity. (Cervical cells are more fragile before the age of eighteen.)
- Contraceptive pills. Use for five years or more may increase risk.
- Smoking.
- Low income/socioeconomic status.
- Family history. Recent research suggests there may be a genetic component that makes it more difficult for an immune system to fight the HPV virus.
- Child of a mother who used DES between 1940 and 1971.
- Compromised immune system such as with HIV or AIDS.
- A diet low in fruits and vegetables. It causes women to miss out on protective antioxidants and phytochemicals known to help prevent cervical cancer.

HPV Vaccines:
Gardasil
- Protects against four types of HPV, including the two types—16 and 18—that cause 70 percent of cervical cancers. The other two types, 6 and 11, cause 90 percent of genital warts.
- Approved for girls and young women ages nine to twenty-six.
- Approved for boys and men ages nine to twenty-six.
Cervarix
- Protects against two types of HPV—16 and 18—that cause 70 percent of cervical cancers.
- Approved for girls and young women ages ten to twenty-five.

Both vaccines
- Recommended for girls ages eleven to twelve.
- Given as a series of three shots.

Ask your doctor if a vaccine is right for you. Note, however, that even if you have received the HPV vaccine, you still need to be screened with the Pap test for cervical cancer. It may still be possible to contract other strains of HPV; the vaccine only protect against certain strains.

Pap Test:
- This is a screening tool used to look for abnormal cells on the cervix that can develop into cervical cancer.
- There are two types of Pap tests: conventional and ThinPrep. The accuracy varies from 50 percent to 80 percent.
- Your first Pap test should be at age twenty-one.
- The American Congress of Obstetricians and Gynecologists (ACOG) recommends a Pap test every three years for women ages twenty-one to twenty-nine.
- ACOG also recommends woman aged thirty or older, with three consecutive negative Pap test be screened once every three years.

HPV Test:
- This is a screening tool used to detect the presence of high-risk HPV, which may lead to present or future abnormal cervical cells.
- Is recommended for women age 21-29 with inconclusive ("ASC-US") Pap test results
- ACOG recommends that women over the age of thirty have a HPV test performed along with their Pap test.
- Having a positive HPV test does not mean you have or will develop cervical cancer. It does mean your health care provider will need to monitor you more closely.

Tips to My Girlfriends ────────────

How to prepare for a gynecological exam:
- Schedule your appointment when you're not menstruating.
- Avoid vaginal medications, lubricants, vaginal contraceptives, and douches for at least forty-eight hours prior to your exam.
- Do not have sexual intercourse for forty-eight hours prior to your exam.
- Remember, your gynecologist is there to help you, not judge you. Tell him/her everything about your sexual behaviors so he/she can give you the proper care. Failure to disclose information can limit your health care provider's ability to properly treat you.
- If you are experiencing pain, problems, or other concerns, record them in a journal so you can give your health care professional detailed information. Note when you experience a problem, what it feels like, what other activities you were engaged in around that time, etc.

Questions to ask your health care provider:
- Am I at risk for HPV?
- How do I protect myself from HPV?
- How often should I have a Pap test?
- What does an abnormal Pap test mean? What will you do next?
- Am I a candidate for the HPV vaccine? Why or why not?
- If I have been vaccinated, do I still need a Pap test? How often?
- Am I a candidate for the HPV test along with my Pap test?
- What does it mean if I have a positive HPV test but a normal Pap test? How will you follow me?
- If I test positive for HPV, will I get cervical cancer?

Questions on Fertility:
- How will my treatment options affect future fertility?
- What are the advantages and disadvantages to freezing embryos instead of freezing eggs? Am I a candidate for either option?

- If my ovaries are left after a hysterectomy and I have recovered from the cancer, can they be safely stimulated for egg retrieval and used with a gestational carrier?
- Does my insurance plan offer any fertility benefits?
- Do I qualify for any studies, discount plans, or nonprofit assistance for fertility treatment?

Other Tips:
- Take another person to the doctor with you when you are receiving results, discussing treatment plans, or making any decisions.
- Health care bills can be overwhelming. Ask a spouse, family member, or friend to help you sort, organize, and juggle them.
- Bad things happen to good people—don't blame yourself.
- You can choose how you respond to life's challenges.
- Even when it's hard, look for the opportunity or the good in your situation.
- Use your experience to educate others around you.
- Remember that you make a difference. Empower yourself.
- Keep your mind open and you might surprise yourself.
- What you think you want may not be what you need. Trust God and the universe to provide and to direct you.

My Tips for Enjoying Sex Again:
- *Talk about it!* Find someone—a partner, friend, therapist, family member, or another survivor—with whom you can be open and honest about your feelings and fears. You have to talk about those feelings and fears to move past them.
- *Let go!* A woman's mind can be her own worst enemy when trying to rekindle sexuality and intimacy. (Think about what your own internal dialogue saying to you?) Trying these techniques to get outside your own head: listen to music, get a massage, take a long hot bath, take a walk, meditate, or enjoy a glass of wine)
- *Seek it out!* It takes work, hard work, before the desire returns. Don't wait on it, go find it. Yes, there will be pain, but this too shall pass.
- *Give yourself permission to be different!* Your experience with cancer has changed you, mind, body, and soul. Explore it all! The greatest levels of intimacy come from breaking down our emotional walls and making ourselves vulnerable to another human being.

- *Explore or rediscover other methods of experiencing intimacy!* Naked cuddle time—kissing, holding, and caressing without the pressure of performing a sexual act—stimulates trust, understanding, intimacy, and eventually desire.
- *Exercise all of your muscles!* Remember the vagina is a muscle. It can shrink from radiation treatment and surgery, but it can be stretched back out for enjoyable sex again (just as it stretches during child birth). Ask your doctor for a set of dilators and use then daily or consider a field trip to your local sex shop. Take your partner with you. It simply takes time. Think of this stretching as your new exercise program. As with any good exercise program, consistency is the key, so stay faithful. Use it or lose it. After the pain will come pleasure.
- *Experiment with lubricants!* Invest in a good lubricant and don't be afraid to use it. (I love Astroglide myself.)
- *Invite him back in!* You probably created boundaries, either consciously or subconsciously, with your partner during your treatment. Remember to invite him back in and give him permission to touch your body. Don't be afraid to provide a little coaching and/or direction. He doesn't know what feels good unless you communicate. If your partner isn't receptive, try sharing ideas over dinner or drinks rather than during the act; no one likes a drill sergeant in bed.
- *Set small goals and practice!* Practice makes perfect. Take it slowly, and don't impose any pressure on yourself. Initially you may only be able to handle penetration for a few minutes. It's okay and normal! Do only what you can. Don't lose hope and don't get discouraged. Practice, practice, practice.
- *Be patient with yourself!* It takes time, but you can achieve great sex again and experience even closer intimacy than you did before!

Tips for Your Partner from Mine:

- *Show your support!* Attend as many doctor and treatment appointments as possible. Even when she tells you that you don't have to, go anyway. This allows you to live the experience with her, and it becomes something you do together.
- *Become a partner and do your own research!* Your level of knowledge and interest in her condition helps you to better understand and cope with what she is experiencing. It also gives her confidence, knowing she can talk to you because you are in it together.

- *Patience is the key!* Know your loved one needs space and permission to cope in her own way. I didn't want my wife to work during chemo and radiation, but she insisted. Every night she came home exhausted and I'd lecture her. What I didn't realize was that although work drained her physically, it uplifted her mentally. Working gave her a reason to keep fighting and made her feel needed. Let your loved one find her own way to cope and then respect her choices.

- *Listen more than you talk and know that you don't have to fix it!* When our loved one is in pain, we often try to fix the problem. Resist this urge. Ask questions and truly listen to what she says. Validate her feelings, even if they seem irrational. Just be her life preserver and flow through the storm with her, knowing the sun will shine again. This act will increase emotional intimacy between the two of you.

- *Be open to taking cues, asking questions, and trying new things!* In the sexual arena, remember to take cues from her. Let her know it is okay to give you direction and that you welcome the feedback. It can be as simple as how to rub her head or feet; or more intimate, like how to touch her in that special place. Let her walk you through exploring her body. Things are different now—be open to learning.

- *Have patience and live in the moment!* Remember, her emotional and psychological scars will linger long after the physical wounds heal, so have patience and take it slow. Find new ways to create intimacy and closeness: cuddle, read together, take bubble baths, give back rubs, try phone sex, etc.

Resource Directory

American Cancer Society
www.cancer.org

Cervical Cancer and HPV Test Info
www.thehpvtest.com

Cervical Cancer Free America
www.cervicalcancerfreeamerica.org

Concerts for a Cure
www.concertsforacure.org

The Digene HPV Test
www.thehpvtest.com

Fertile Action
www.fertileaction.org

Fertile Hope
www.fertilehope.org

Foundation for Women's Cancers
(formerly Gynecological Cancer Foundation)
www.foundationforwomenscancer.org

The Hicks Foundation
http://www.freepap.org

Hyster Sisters
www.hystersisters.org

Immerman Angels
www.Immermanangels.org

The KristenForbes EVE Foundation
www.Kristeneve.org

My Life Line
www.mylifeline.org

National Cervical Cancer Coalition
www.nccc-online.org

Partnership to End Cervical Cancer
www.nocervicalcancer.org

Pearl of Wisdom Campaign to End Cervical Cancer
www.PearlofWisdom.us

SAS Cervical Cancer Foundation
www.sasfoundation.org

Say Something
www.saysomething.org

Tamika and Friends Inc.
www.tamikaandfriends.com

Women's Cancer Network
www.wcn.org

The Yellow Umbrella Organization
www.theyellowumbrella.org

Printed in the United States
By Bookmasters